A Slice of the TIMES

Kansas City 1875 - 1880

Brad Finch

Articles reprinted with the permission of the
Kansas City STAR

Second printing, September, 1995

ISBN 0-9645325-0-6

To my brother Doug, who has a way of making things happen. And to my wife Jennifer, for everything else.

Contents

On the south side of Fifth Street between Main and Delaware, circa 1880

Preface

Most history books focus on the major developments in a time period and tend to ignore, either because of structural limitations or perceived unimportance, the idiosyncrasies of the culture. Questions such as, what was important to them, what did they find humorous, what did they do for entertainment, in essence, what were their lives like, are rarely addressed. In this case, no people survive to provide the answers, so the next best resources are the newspapers of the time.

This book reproduces selected news stories, in their entirety, which appeared in the consecutive columns entitled Street Gossip, Town Topics, Home News and City Summary, in the Kansas City Times from January of 1875 through December of 1880. These columns were a collection of news trivia concerning the day to day happenings in the city. The stories were never any longer than one paragraph and contained events rarely recorded anywhere else.

The research for this collection took over six months and required the reading of an estimated 40,000 individual news stories in an effort to provide a representation of the times. Regular readers of history will probably find the format of this book unusual. Instead of telling the reader what has been revealed in the research, you are allowed to discover it for yourself, in true form and chronological context. It is akin to opening a small window on a time period more than 120 years ago, and peering in. Some of the articles reproduced here are humorous, some are sad, but all should be enlightening.

Before the "Boom"

The period 1875 - 1880 is one of the most overlooked stages of Kansas City's history. Most books on the subject just skim through or skip the period altogether. Understandable when you consider the fact that this is only six years in a span of over 150 years to cover. But this brief period has a lot to reveal for those who care to dig deeper.

Kansas City in 1875 had a self-described "out-at-elbows" appearance owing to its haphazard beginnings. Only a few roads had yet been macadamized, or gravel covered, and sidewalks, where there were any, were usually wood-planked. Residences were built in close proximity to retail stores, manufacturing plants, grain elevators, foundries and packing houses, in many cases, just next door. What zoning laws there were allowed for the sale of lots as small as 25 front feet wide; a size more easily adapted to the grouping together of multiple lots for commercial use later. Regular re-grading and widening of the streets pushed sidewalks up to the front doors of many buildings and required the relocation of others.

The average day-laborer's wage of $1.00 to $1.50 per day made owning a home nearly impossible. Although some still managed to build their own houses, the majority of homes were built as rental property by the more affluent members of the city. Many hotels not only accommodated travelers, but also provided permanent residents with long-term living arrangements. One of few exceptions to these living conditions was "Quality Hill" on the bluffs overlooking the west bottoms, where the "upper walks of life" built large, beautiful brick residences for themselves.

A Slice of the TIMES

The boundaries of the City of Kansas (as it was officially known) during the period 1875 through 1880 ran from 23rd Street to the south, the Missouri river to the north, the state line to the west and Woodland Avenue to the east. This seemingly small area contained a wide spectrum humanity. Muggers, prostitutes, pickpockets, burglars and disreputable gamblers provided an air of unease among residents, and unwelcome surprises for travelers. Transportation within the city was provided by horse or mule drawn trolley cars and numerous hacks. Livestock such as cows, pigs, chickens, and goats could be seen wandering freely throughout the city despite ordinances requiring their containment. This plus an estimated population of over 40,000, not counting the hundreds of emigrants passing through daily via the railroads and the Union Depot, made for the kind of experience most would rather forget.

But it was during this period in Kansas City's history that some of the most important and sweeping changes were made, building the groundwork for this "city of the future." The introduction of a system of waterworks for Kansas City in 1875 brought with it the first ornamental water fountains, lawn sprinklers and drinking fountains, as well as improved fire fighting abilities. This period saw Kansas City's first city-owned public park, and the planning of it's first Boulevard (although it should be mentioned that it may not have met the criteria we associate with the Boulevards of today). Efforts to clean up the city led to the creation of the first Board of Health department, a system of sewerage and the city's first impounder. New hospitals were started while older ones improved. The building boom that began during this time laid the foundation for the city's architectural identity. Craftsmen like Asa

Before the "Boom"

Beebe Cross planned some of the most appealing public and private structures the city had ever seen, a few of which still stand today. It was during this period that Kansas City was looking for more than just to survive as a community, and began to take on metropolitan aspirations.

Kaw Water
1875

1875 was a pivotal year for Kansas City. The National Waterworks Company of New York had been hired by Kansas City to build a pumping station on the banks of the Kaw River and had finished laying the first of many water mains and fire hydrants to provide the City with her first central water system. Kaw water was the logical choice. Not only was the Missouri River too muddy to use (although some people of the time insisted that a little Missouri mud was good for you), the "Big Muddy" was also the last stop for waste from the meat packing plants on the western edge of the city. Before this time, all citizens relied on numerous wells and springs for their drinking and cleaning water. The Fire Department continued to rely on a system of cisterns dug throughout the city which had to be refilled after pumping water out to douse fires.

1875 also brought a new charter for the City of Kansas. One of the most notable provisions of this charter, imposed by the state of Missouri, required the city to limit its spending to no more money than it was collecting. At this time the city was operating under a municipal debt of nearly one and a half million dollars while the rate of taxation was relatively high at 22 mills, or 2.2 cents on the dollar. This put the city in a bind, leading to severe cutbacks in city services, and leaving creditors like the National Waterworks Co. wondering if they would be paid.

The year was marked by a repeat of last year's grasshopper plague which threatened crops in both Missouri and Kansas, pushing the city council toward actions similar to the farm subsidies of today.

Nationally, Congress passed the Civil Rights Act, guaranteeing African Americans equal access to public places, hotels, restaurants, theaters, etc. It was never enforced, and was ruled unconstitutional in 1883.

A Slice of the TIMES

-This cold weather is what is needed if the ice men are to gather a supply of ice for next summer.
January 1

-The married men employed by the TIMES were each presented with a turkey last evening. It took 21 gobblers to go the rounds.
January 1

-Four hundred more Menonites are on the way from New York to their new home in Kansas. These people are the most thrifty in the world, and will make good citizens in whatever country they may settle.
January 1

-A wagon loaded heavily with wood, and owned by a man from Westport, met in deadly strife with the horse rail-road track near Bluff street yesterday afternoon. The wagon came out second best, and caused the owner thereof to swear in at least four languages.
January 1

-Mr. C.O. Tichener, who some time since obtained a judgment against the City on a certificate of indebtedness for $226, yesterday served an attachment on the instruments of the City Engineer's office. Judge Dillon, some months since, decided a case wherein the points were the same, in the negative, and will probably do the same with this.
January 1

-The alarm of fire early yesterday morning called the Fire Department to the Fourth ward to put out a fire that had broken out in a building just on the State line near the stock yards. The department responded quickly to the summons, but found that no water could be brought to bear on the burning building, the hydrants being too far away; so had to stand by and see the building burn down. The house - a two story one - belonged to a Mr. A. J. Snider, and was valued at $800. The fire is supposed to have been the work of an incendiary, as the same building was set on fire about a month since. It was formerly occupied by a saloon-keeper named Porter, but at the time of the fire was unoccupied. The loss is partially covered by insurance.

January 1

-George Passmore, a white man, was married to a colored woman named Mrs. John Snith, in West Kansas, last Saturday evening. A colored minister did the business for them, and the four little children of Mrs. Passmore *nee* Snith furnished fun on the occasion.

January 5

West Kansas is a sub-division of Kansas City, Missouri in the West Bottoms near the river.

A Slice of the TIMES

-It was amusing to see an insurance agent rushing around, the night of the fire, for some one to open a fire plug. In the Council he favored a resolution instructing the Chief of the Fire Department not to use the water from the hydrants under any consideration until the city accepted it. Personal interest has a wonderful influence.
January 6

-The new lodging-room for homeless unfortunates furnished by the city is nightly filled. Last night 28 inmates enjoyed the hospitality of the comfortable quarters.
January 8

-Charles Vindquest, while cutting ice yesterday, froze one of his hands quite severely. He is of the opinion that yesterday was the coldest day the people of Kansas City ever experienced.
January 9

-The men employed in cutting ice about the city were yesterday compelled to discontinue their labors on account of the weather. At 1:30 o'clock on Grand avenue the mercury dropped down to 4° below zero, and on Main street at the same hour the thermometer indicated 6°.
January 9

Kaw Water - 1875

-Had it not been that the firemen had filled a cistern from a fire-plug on the night of the fire in the Grand Central Hotel, that splendid block would to-day be in ruins. When the flames seemed to be getting beyond control, the water in both cisterns from which the engines were pumping was found to be exhausted. Then it was that one of the engineers, disregarding the orders which had been issued, opened a fire-plug and supplied the water, without which the building would surely have been destroyed. The firemen, above all others, appreciate the manifold system of water-works.
January 10

-Mike Callaghan was fooling with a young bull dog at Engine House No. 1, yesterday, and got bit in the nose.
January 16

-It is curious that a head of blonde hair can't go down the street after dark without turning everybody else's head. This is one of the cases where one turn doesn't deserve another. You can turn your nose at this if you like; but the turn which affairs are taking in this line has turned the attention of the best people in society to the TIMES to have it stopped.
January 26

-"What is the matter with the gas?" asked a nervous individual, last night. "Don't know," was the reply; "we're all in the dark on that subject."
February 12

-An enterprising salesman in a popular clothing house on Main street, rather than lose a customer last night, while the gas was out, selected an overcoat by a lighted match, and taking it to an adjoining store where kerosene was used, closed the bargain.
February 12

-A locomotive yesterday ran over an ambitious young member of the genus swine, which was loafing around the Union depot. Any one but a hog would commence an action for damages.
February 12

-Mah-yaw-aw-pet and Pash-she-paw-ho, chiefs of the Fox and Sac Indian tribes, were at the Union depot yesterday, on their way home from a visit to Washington, where they have been negotiating with the government for a change of location. They will advise their tribes to remove to the Indian Nation.
February 13

-On Friday one of the water pipes on Sixteenth street, corner of Walnut, burst, while the mains were being tested, and overflowed the stables of Irwin Bros. with about 18 inches of water, and the building has settled in several places from three to six inches. The Irwin Brothers propose to claim damages from the Waterworks Company.
February 23

-Muddy sidewalks and soiled stockings were fashionable yesterday.

February 23

-There will be a preliminary test of the water works to-day, and on Saturday or Monday the final test will occur. At 3 o'clock this afternoon streams will be thrown at the same time from the following places: Corners of Fourth and Main; Fifth and Walnut; Ninth and Harrison; Twelfth and Locust; Sixteenth and Main; Sixteenth and Locust; Sixteenth and Catherine; Thirteenth and Penn; Tenth and Broadway; Ninth and Delaware; Twelfth and Liberty; and opposite the Union Depot.

February 23

-Tom Weston was out testing the water mains on Monday. He had applied the gauge to a hydrant, and, stooping over it, was watching the needle carefully as it was pushed away up to 185. Suddenly the main burst, and a large column of water coming up from the ground raised Weston and sent him sprawling half way over the street. He is of the opinion that this testing process has been applied to him as well as the pipes.

February 25

-Fifth street, at Broadway, is in deplorable condition, the mud being fully six inches deep, and no crossings on either side of Broadway. The cry goes up from those who have to travel that way, and

the TIMES calls upon the proper authorities to build a crossing immediately, as in no other part of the city is one more badly needed.
March 12

-The police have done some good work in ferreting out the gang of thieves which have been operating in the city so long. Some second-hand dealers seem to be concerned in the robberies.
March 16

-The river is freezing over again.
March 17

-The ice dealer isn't having just the kind of weather to please him. He had enough of the zero business last January.
March 17

-Blustering breezes raised the sand from the banks of the river yesterday and sent dense clouds of it whirling over the city.
March 17

-Wilson Askew has no more taste for duck hunting. On Thursday he went out with his father to shoot ducks on Turkey creek, and the old man left him at a certain point, telling him to remain until he returned. But Wils didn't stay more than 20 minutes, and assigns as the reason that the creek froze over in that time and he couldn't stand the cold, so he

wended his way home, leaving his parental ancestor in the woods looking for his boy. The old gentleman got six ducks.
March 20

-Forcade thinks Kaw water will do for him. He is having the pipes put in and will have the water inside by to-night.
March 26

-Mr. A. H. Halleck has offered to adopt a small child, who for the last few weeks has been cruelly beaten by a drunken mother.
March 28

-A young fellow named Emery, from La Cygne, Kansas, while at the Union Depot night before last, was confidencedout of $60 by a man who represented himself as a ticket agent. He offered him three twenty gold dollar pieces, and the lad handed over the greenbacks, thinking it would be a nice thing to have some of the "yellow boys" about him. He got them, but soon found that they were bogus, and now he has more faith than ever in rag money. He continued his journey yesterday for California. No arrests have been made.
March 28

-Over two hundred California emigrants passed through the city yesterday.
April 2

A Slice of the TIMES

-The Waterworks Company are putting in numerous street sprinklers in various parts of the city.
April 2

-Four brothers from Massachusetts named Forrest were at the Stock Yards yesterday afternoon making inquiries for native cows to take with them to Colorado, where they propose to embark in the stock raising business.
April 2

-Under the amended charter every citizen is requested to leave at the City Assessor's office on or before May 10, a list of all taxable property owned by them on February 15, and a statement of the highest amount of merchandise in their possession between the 15th day of November, 1874, and the 15th day of February, 1875. Failing to do this the citizen is liable to a fine of $100.
April 3

-Old Uncle John, a former slave of the McGee family, was yesterday turned out of the shanty on the corner of Seventeenth and Cherry streets, where he has resided for many years. The property had been sold by Mrs. Vincent and the purchaser intends building. Old John was offered about $10 to move peaceably, but the officers had to be brought into requisition.
April 4

Kaw Water - 1875

-Mattie Sneed was brought before the Recorder yesterday for the fourth time charged with being an inmate in a house of prostitution. She was fined $28.25 and sent to the workhouse.
April 15

-The necessary repairs on the Missouri river bridges will cost the snug little sum of seventeen thousand five hundred dollars. The American Bridge Company of Chicago have the contract for the repairs.
April 15

-Repairs are now being made all along the Westport street car line, and Superintendent Holmes is sparing no effort to make this road all that can be desired by the traveling public. The 5-cent fare is rapidly increasing the number of passengers over the line, and with beer gardens open on Sundays more cars will have to be put on to accommodate the public.
April 17

-One hundred forty-five foot telegraph poles arrived here from Chicago on six flat cars, yesterday. They were consigned to Sol Palmer, chief of construction, Western Union Telegraph Company, and are to be used in rebuilding the lines throughout the city.
April 21

A Slice of the TIMES

-The latest thing out is a manufactured corn-cob pipe. A tobacco house on the Avenue received a consignment of them yesterday, and they sell like hot cakes.
April 23

-The ground in the Exposition Grounds is literally swarming with young grasshoppers.
April 23

-Messrs. A. J. Snider, M. H. Dickenson, E. H. Brooks and D. Underwood will leave the city this morning for a days hunt in the swamps below Independence. Snipe is the attraction.
April 24

-Early yesterday morning a stranger entered a saloon on Main street and asked the privilege of washing his face, which was covered with blood. His request was granted, and after the ablution was performed he departed without making any explanations.
April 24

-Insurance men are never at a loss for an argument. Before the water-works were established, rates were high because there was a scarcity of water, and now that there is plenty, rates are high because the abundance of water will do great damage to goods in case of fire.
April 24

16

-The Vienna Garden will soon put up an elegant fountain-the first in the city.
April 24
The Vienna Garden was located on the Southwest corner of Walnut and Missouri Ave.

-Several lawn sprinklers - really very handsome fountains - have been ordered by citizens.
April 24

-Judge Jenkins will deliver a lecture this evening before the Philomathian Society, at the High School building, corner of Eleventh and Locust streets. Subject: "The age we live in."
April 29

-A negro dance-house on Grand avenue, has become a source of great annoyance to the residents of that quarter, and the police have been notified in regard to the matter.
May 2

-Work will be begun next week on the new St. Patrick's church, located on the corner of Eighth and Cherry streets. It will when completed be one of the finest church edifices in the city.
May 2
This building still stands and is in use as the oldest church building in Kansas City.

A Slice of the TIMES

-Morton, 724 Main Street, is at his old tricks again dealing out the most delicious lemonade and ice cream that ever passed mortal lips. The lemonade is made of pure spring water. Try them.
May 7

-In tearing down the old foundation of St. Patrick's church, which was built some years ago by a contractor named Smith, the workmen have found the inside of the walls filled with small broken rock thrown in without plaster or cement. Not a stone has yet been found which reached entirely through the wall, and competent builders say that had the church proper been erected on such a foundation, the whole thing would have tumbled down. How many of our public buildings are put up in such an unsafe manner?
May 7

-The steamer Kate Kinney was up yesterday.
May 8

-The steamer Joe Chambers passed up this morning.
May 8

-And still the rush continues. A large party of California emigrants passed through yesterday.
May 8

18

-Bellchambers & Co., broom manufacturers, received a car load of broom corn yesterday which cost them over $1,000. Think of it, farmers of Missouri and Kansas, and put in a patch of broom corn as an experiment.
May 9

-Six well equipped emigrant wagons passed through this city yesterday on their way to Kansas. The owners are evidently not afraid of the grasshoppers.
May 9

-Street sprinkling has become fashionable pastime and the dust hasn't much of a show where the waterworks hydrants are opened.
May 13

-Mr. Charles Carlat will re-open the old Gilliss House to-night (Thursday) with a grand ball and other festivities. Good music will be in attendance.
May 13

-Grasshoppers are doing great damage at Liberty.
May 18

-Grasshoppers are grieving over the poor prospect for food since the grass has disappeared.
May 18

-Cattle are dying near Hickman's Mills - pasturage eaten up by the voracious grasshopper.
May 18

A Slice of the TIMES

-A band of wandering Bohemians or Gypsies arrived in the city yesterday from Kansas, and are encamped on Grand Avenue near Twentieth street.
May 22

-A St. Joe girl the other day ate four pounds of wedding cake in order that she might dream of her future husband. And now she says that money wouldn't hire her to marry the fellow she saw in that dream.
May 22

-Pretty nearly the entire population of Independence was engaged yesterday fighting the grasshoppers. County Clerk Hickman had a ditch about one hundred yards long in which he estimated he has destroyed over fifty bushels of the pestiferous insects.
May 23

By late May, the grasshopper plague had become so bad that on May 26 the TIMES began a new column, in the same format as Street Gossip, to relay the tales of the grasshopper problem and citizen's efforts to thwart them. What follows are excerpts from that first column of May 26, titled:

*   *   *   *   *   *   *

GRASSHOPPERANTICS

-Mr. Wilson of Independence avenue and Holmes street, has encircled his entire place with trenches, and is happy in the replanting of his garden.

Kaw Water - 1875

-Over in Lathrop they pay a dollar a bushel for dead red legs.

-O.K. creek is fairly dammed with dead grasshoppers of all ages.

-Quality Hill is at last invaded and the upper walks of life are exceedingly animated.

-A large delegation of grasshoppers presented themselves at the Union Ticket Office yesterday and inquired the distance to Grasshopper Falls.

-Forest avenue folks have used up about all the old mops in that vicinity in making kerosene-saturated torches to make it red-hot for the hoppers.

-The grasshoppers were at the telegraph office yesterday with a view to ascertaining the condition of the crops in Iowa, Illinois and Eastern Missouri.

-A champion fire extinguisher charged with blue vitriol, coal oil, asafoetida, and several other fatal ingredients were used to exterminate grasshoppers yesterday on 6th street without effect.

*   *   *   *   *   *   *

-The first sale of the season of through Texan cattle was effected yesterday at the Stock Yards. The lot consisted of 41 cows averaging 734 pounds and sold for $2.70 per cwt.

May 27

21

A Slice of the TIMES

-Engine No. 2 and the gallant firemen were photographed yesterday.
June 1

-The grasshoppers gathered in full force on the curbstones yesterday to watch the circus go by.
June 1

-The stench from dead grasshoppers in the eastern part of the city is very unpleasant.
June 1

-It is a literal fact that the head of a grasshopper can be removed from the body and then be replaced, and a few moments after the hopper goes about his business almost as lively as ever. This operation was gone through with yesterday by several curious parties in this office and the TIMES has now quite a cabinet of the improved insects, the only difficulty found in their management being the curbing of their appetite in eating each other up. Catch a healthy hopper, cut his head off with a sharp knife and then put it back carefully and see how it is for yourself.
June 15

-Mrs. Haley, of West Kansas, illuminated her stove with kerosene yesterday and now she won't have a photograph taken till the wounds heal.
June 25

-Spruce beer and straw hats are all the style this hot weather.
June 26

-Superintendent Greenwood reports that 84 scholars have passed examinations for the High School, and that all the schools have not yet been heard from. The whole number will exceed 100.
June 26

-J. H. Mantzing was arraigned yesterday and fined for infringing the ice ordinance. He tried to keep cool, but he couldn't help exclaiming (sarcastically) that it was an ice law that inflicted such penalties.
June 26
The ice ordinance, as it was called, required that all ice wagons be licensed.

-The police made a raid about ten o'clock last night on a house of prostitution kept by a colored woman back of the Journal building. The inmates, five in number, were placed in the cooler.
June 29

-The final meeting of the relief committee will be held this afternoon. Two thousand eight hundred people have received assistance.
June 29

-Grasshoppers were flying yesterday in countless numbers.
June 30

A Slice of the TIMES

-The Plug-Uglies scooped in the Nose-Crackers in a game of base ball, over in Hell's Half Acre yesterday.
July 6
"Hell's Half Acre" was an area of the West Bottoms bounded by Santa Fe Street on the east, the State Line on the west, 9th Street on the south, and roughly 7th Street on the north.

-In time the Brown Stocking ball nine from this city may play a second-rate game of ball. Yesterday the White Socks walked away with them by a score of 93 to 25. They would have made the other seven runs, but one of the players lived in Wyandotte, and wanted to go home.
July 6

-The Waterworks displayed something of their ability Monday, as to what they could do in case of a fire. Two magnificent streams were thrown from the corner of Fourth and Main, and two were thrown on the ruins of Whittaker's building. The remnants of the roof and the toppling walls were torn from their fastenings and hurled with a crash to the ground by the mighty force of the water as it was forced out - 120 pounds pressure to the square inch.
July 7

-The corner-stone of the new Catholic church on the corner of Eighth and Cherry streets will be laid by Bishop Ryan on Sunday the 25th of this month.
July 7
Rain prevented that ceremony on July 25. It was rescheduled for August 22 and went off without a hitch.

-Mr. Whittaker, with true Kansas City pluck, commenced removing the debris preparatory to rebuilding his three-story building, which was destroyed by fire on Monday.
July 7

-The new synagogue being built by the Israelites of this city, upon the corner of Sixth and Wyandotte streets, is fast assuming commanding proportions. It will be one of the neatest church edifices in the city.
July 9
This new building was built by the B'nai Jehudah congregation, who until this time, had been using the nearby Unitarian Church to meet in.

-The City Engineer is respectfully requested by the business men to see to the removal of the filth at the corner of Fifth and Delaware streets. Kaw water may be good enough fresh from the pipes, but it certainly smells loud after the hogs have wallowed in it for a few days.
July 9

-Twelve streams were thrown by the Waterworks yesterday, averaging 120 feet in height, 20 feet above what the contract requires; and that too from a six inch main in the part of the city most distant from the pumps, and where it was thought impossible to be done. The measure of the streams was made by City Engineer Holmes.
July 10

-The water thrown yesterday all came from the upper distributing reservoir, and the machinery was not employed to one-tenth of its capacity.
July 10

Main pumping station on the bank of the Kaw River, circa 1875.

Kaw Water - 1875

On July 13, 1875, the TIMES changed the name of the Street Gossip column to Town Topics. The column retained both its form and content.

-The Jackson County Horse Railway Company will, in a few days, commence the joining together of the Forest avenue and Twelfth street lines, thus making a complete circuit or belt. When in full working order cars will be run the entire circuit, three one way and three the other, thus doubling the accommodation, as points on either line will be accessible from both directions. This decidedly important enterprise will be hailed with genuine pleasure by the many who depend upon the cars for their daily transportation.
July 13

-As usual at this season of the year croakers frighten weak-minded folks by yelling mad dog.
July 13

-Two thousand citizens have signed and sent to the Police Commissioners a protest against the reduction of the pay of policemen.
July 13

-Real estate in the city is looking up, the brighter aspect of things in general and the presence here of two or three capitalists who are buying largely, having the tendency to make the market more

hopeful than it has been at any time for a year or more. A Florida gentleman now owns the Kansas City National Bank building.
July 13

-A number of boys were arrested yesterday afternoon by Officer Sandford for bathing in the Missouri river, against which there is a city ordinance. They had been warned a number of times not to do it, but paid no attention to what was said, and now are in the cooler.
July 14

-There is some talk of changing the location of the City Hospital to a more accessible point on McGee street.
July 15

-Two thousand and seventy-four males, two thousand one hundred and eighty-eight females, or four thousand two hundred and sixty-two children all told, was the average attendance at the public schools last year vide the annual report.
July 15

-Thermometer at 104° yesterday.
July 16

-The appearance of the circus tent yesterday afternoon was certainly anything but suggestive of grasshopper times.
July 21

-It is really astonishing to observe how many grown people it invariably requires to take one little child to a show.

July 21

-The chronic mud holes just opposite Union Depot have been treated to a heavy load of stones and are now much better. Thank you.

July 21

-The first batch of wild pigeons - 350 - for the pigeon shooting tournament on the 29th and 30th, will arrive this morning. They come from Chicago where 1,500 in all were purchased, being shipped in lots in order to receive better care and escape wholesale mortality.

July 22

-New oats from Johnson county, Kansas, to the extent of nine wagon loads, were sold on the public square yesterday. The grain was of superior quality, yielding forty bushels to the acre. And yet but little over a month ago the report from Johnson county was to the effect that the grasshoppers had chewed it clean up.

July 22

-The various ponds about the city are in fearful condition, and unless the authorities soon awake to the emergency, much sickness will be the result thereof.

July 29

A Slice of the TIMES

-The Waterworks test on Quality Hill yesterday afternoon was quite a feature of attraction to the West Enders, the streams arising many feet above the summit of the bluffs, and forming beautiful rainbows.

July 29

-Architect Cross has returned from Cottonwood Falls, where he went to examine the building stone taken from a large quarry in that vicinity with the view of making a contract for a supply sufficient to build the new St. Patrick's church, in case the trustees decide to build of stone instead of brick. He declares himself immensely pleased with the quality of the stone, it being much harder than that of Junction City, of a better color, being somewhat darker, and in every way the equal of the Warrensburg stone. Its cost is also a very attractive feature, as it can be put on the cars at 15 cents to 60 cents for Warrensburg. It can be laid down here for 35 cents, and the cost of building the church of it would be but $2,000 more than brick.

August 3

-No less than six cows have been poisoned in West Kansas within the past two or three days, and if the parties who are so recklessly destroying the milkers are ever caught it will go hard with them, sure.

August 3

-An ambitious stone thrower played the duce with one of the large plate glass windows at Menown's tea store, corner of Main and Fifth street Sunday afternoon. He was bent upon distancing the best efforts of a boot black and succeeded at a cost of $200.
August 3

-Yesterday was a memorable day with the colored folks of the city, it being widely observed as the fifteenth anniversary of the emancipation of slaves in the West Indies. A monster picnic was held on the Exposition Grounds, and at night a grand ball at Long's Hall.
August 3

-Never before in the history of this city has the mortality among children been as great as at the present time.
August 5

-A movement is on foot looking to the establishment of a hospital by the Sisters connected with St. Teresa's Academy, and it is to be hoped it will be successful, as a good hospital is much needed.
August 5

-Upwards of one hundred and twenty-five men are now employed in the works of construction at the new rolling mills. The foundation is all in, some of

the machinery placed, and it is expected that work will be formally commenced about the first of October.
August 11

-After the great scare over the grasshoppers in May and June, the predictions of famine and relief fund subscribed, it appears odd to refer to the Exposition entry of a ten acre field of corn by a Jackson county man. Nevertheless such is the fact.
August 13

-The monument destined for the grave of ex-Mayor McGee has arrived, and will be placed in position with Masonic ceremonies on Sunday.
August 14

The Mayor was Col. Elijah Milton McGee, an early landowner in K. C. In 1856 he platted McGee's Addition, from 12th Street South, from Main to Holmes, and named many of the streets after members of his family. He was buried in McGee's Cemetery, but later moved to Elmwood Cemetery.

-Not a murder for a year, not a suicide all summer, nor a scandal fully developed for months, and yet people do say that it is strange newspaper men do not present columns fairly teeming with exciting local news. But for the railroad war there is no telling what might have happened to reporters.
August 14

The following article from the St. Louis Globe - Democrat of August 13, was reprinted in the Town Topics column August 14.

Kansas City has a little scheme for getting rid of her sick and destitute, which she is practicing at the expense of St. Louis. It is all very well in its way, and may be looked upon as a credible proceeding in that locality, but the chances are that it will not meet with general favor. Owing to competition between two Kansas City railway lines, the rate of fare has been reduced to $2.50 to this point, and in view of this Kansas City officials are shipping their destitute hospital cases to St. Louis for care and treatment. No less than a dozen called at the City Dispensary yesterday for permits, many of the cases being very severe. Each one had his story to tell about applying to the Kansas City authorities for help, but instead of receiving it was furnished transportation to St. Louis, and directed to call upon the hospital authorities here. In the rules governing the Dispensary, no provision is made for this class of cases, and in the Kansas City officials forwarding them here, it is getting rid of care at the expense of humanity, for these applicants, unless their illness be of the severest type, must go without treatment.

-There seems to be little doubt but that Deputy Collector Randal has absconded. A letter was received from him yesterday by Collector

Anderson, but nothing was learned as to his whereabouts. His accounts are said to be over $1,000 short.
August 26

-The delinquent taxes of Kansas City amount to the snug little sum of $400,000.
August 28

-The new uniform for members of the Fire Department is to consist of a blue shirt and dark pants.
August 28

-A meeting of prominent property owners on "Quality Hill" was held last Saturday night, to protest against the proposed erection of a hospital on the site of the Waterman place on Penn street. The protest is based on the opinion of several medical gentlemen, who state that the erection of such an institution in that place will prove detrimental to the health of the city.
August 31

-An attempt is being made to get the Sisters to exchange their property on Penn street for the Phillips property on Delaware street, near Central and Sixteenth street. In the event of failure to do this the committee will propose to purchase the Southern Hotel on Grand avenue and offer it in exchange for the Penn street property. Anything to get rid of the hospital.
September 3

Kaw Water - 1875

-The ice men are praying for a continuance of the hot weather.
September 8

-Two youngsters, one white and the other colored, were fined $5.25 each for fighting the day before yesterday. Will this war of races never end?
September 8

-The topic of most general and exiting interest in this community at the present time is not Barnum's Hippodrome nor the Exposition. It is the mosquito. There is not a house in town that is not nightly raided by this pestiferous little insect. In many places they are so numerous and voracious as to render life almost a burden. Old settlers assert that they are more numerous now than they have ever been before. Merchants say there has been double the call for netting this season. The druggists say there has been a perfect rush for oil of pennyroyal, carbolic acid and other supposed panaceas for the poisonous stings of mosquitos. One gentleman who reports his domestic life as pleasant as usually falls to the lot mortals, insists that mosquitos have almost divided his family. His wife calls for pennyroyal, burnt rags, burnt camphor, carbolic acid all night long. He says he has tried all remedies yet suggested, and still he is the victim of savage and continuous attacks from this light muscled insect.
September 10

A Slice of the TIMES

-The banks and principal business houses were closed during the larger portion of the day yesterday, to give the clerks and employees opportunity to attend the Exposition.
September 17

-Peter Muehleback; of Westport, the enterprising and successful manufacturer of native wines, had a very fine display of a number of varieties of wine at the late imposition. He received a number of blue ribbons and diplomas.
September 19
Peter Muehlbach became so successful that in 1878 he built a large wine garden adjacent to his thirty-three acre vineyard and farm at 41st Street and State Line. It remained in operation until prohibition closed it forever.

-The City Engineer and the Secretary of the Water Works are writing letters to each other on the subject of having another "test". In the mean-time fires occur, and Waterworks are not used until the buildings are burned.
September 23
At about 2:30 AM Sept. 22, fire was discovered at the Chicago House directly across the street from the Union Depot. The fire grew out of control and Union Depot, as well as the Chicago House and other surrounding buildings, were destroyed.

-The new depot is likely to be located on or near the site of the old one.
September 23

-The work of clearing away the rubbish at the depot is going on rapidly, and will soon be entirely accomplished.
September 24

-It is stated that Col. Coates made it a condition of sale of the land on which the Union Depot is now located, that it should be occupied as a general passenger depot.
September 24

-The railroad officials propose to enclose the shed at the Union Depot and use it as a temporary depot and waiting room. No building will be put up at present on the site of the old depot.
September 24

-One hundred and seventy-six head of cattle direct from New Mexico, via A., T. & S. F., were sold at the Kansas Stock Yards yesterday. Who says Kansas City isn't becoming a great cattle market?
September 28

-There are 232 pupils enrolled in the High School. During the first month last year there were but 140.
October 1

-There are one hundred and fifty colored pupils in the primary department of the colored school. A pretty fair basis for an increase in the colored vote.
October 1

A Slice of the TIMES

-A man named Ellis, from Indiana, accompanied by a colored man, went into a certain hotel in the city yesterday and wanted dinner for himself and companion. When told by the proprietor that the colored man could not eat at the same table with white folks, Ellis got wrathy and threatened to sue the hotel for damages. After a good deal of talk and excitement the civil rights bill triumphed.
October 7

-A new kind of concrete sidewalk was being laid on Missouri avenue yesterday.
October 9

-The Sister's Hospital was yesterday opened for the first time to patients. Dr. Boarman took one there during the day.
October 17
Despite efforts by the City and the residents of Quality Hill, the Sister's of Saint Teresa's opened their hospital on the Southwest corner of Seventh and Pennsylvania. They named it St. Joseph's Hospital.

-Over two hundred car loads of cattle were received at the Kansas City stock yards yesterday.
October 20

-The last steamer of the season, from St. Louis, the Fannie Lewis, arrived at the levee yesterday morning. She had a full cargo, the bulk of which was consigned to this city.
October 20

-Persons all over the city should look to it that their back doors are all safely bolted before retiring for the night. Sneak thieves are around and carry off everything that comes in their way.
October 22

-Fannie Clark and Kate Donahue were each fined $4.25 yesterday morning for calling each other hard names.
October 22

-The burning of a defective flue out at the Southern Hotel, on Grand avenue, caused an alarm of fire about seven o'clock last night. Just before the alarm was given Andy Scanlan, foreman of No. 3 on Missouri avenue, was talking to a St. Louis man in regard to the time it took the engines to get out of the engine house. The St. Louis man stated that he had seen the engines in his city get out in two minutes and a half. Andy told him he could go him two minutes better, and before he had gotten the words out of his mouth the alarm was given, and by the watch, it took just thirty-four seconds time to get the horses hitched up and the engine out on the street on its way to the fire. The St. Louis man vamoosed and has not been seen since.
October 28

-A member of the School Board yesterday stated, that since the introduction of Kaw water into the school buildings, children did not find it necessary

to carry water in bottles from home, which was a common occurrence before the pipe connections were made.
October 31

-All jurors were discharged by Judge Sawyer, of the Circuit Court, on Thursday at noon, and since that time his Honor has been kept busy granting injunctions restraining the City Tax Collector from selling property on which taxes for some reason or the other had not been paid. Over one hundred such injunctions were granted on Friday and nearly as many more yesterday. People all over the city are waking up to the fact that the Collector means business, and unless taxes are paid the property will be sold.
October 31

-Injunctions are being granted by Judge Sawyer, of the Circuit Court, at the rate of a dozen an hour.
November 2

-Captain Baldwin with detachment of U.S. troops passed through the city last night from Fort Leavenworth, on his way to Jefferson City. It is well known that for some time military prisoners convicted of crime have been taken to the Missouri capital for safe keeping, but now that the prison at the Fort has been finished and considered the safer place, all prisoners are to be removed to it from the

State prison. Captain Baldwin will return to Leavenworth with the last of the culprits on Wednesday.
November 2

-The city tax collector continued the sale of property yesterday morning at nine o'clock. After disposing of 17 feet from the south side of lot seven, block "B", Ranson & Talley's addition, for $3.21, the sale was postponed. Tax payers are coming up and settling just as fast as the papers can be made out and the taxes on nearly half the property advertised as delinquent will be paid before time of sale.
November 5

-Complaint is being made on all sides that the gas throughout the city is "doused" at to early an hour in the morning. Passengers for the early trains state that on Fifth from Main to the depot every lamp is put out long before it is daylight, and in consequence they have to grope their way along as best they can. A pedestrian stated to a TIMES reporter yesterday that he went into the gutter opposite the City Hotel, on Tuesday morning, and for a few seconds had a little circus all to himself in trying to get on his pins again. The proper authorities would do well to look into the matter.
November 6

A Slice of the TIMES

-A large number of people pass through the city daily on their way back from California, where they had gone with the intention of buying land and settling. Yesterday morning a party of 25 came in on the Council Bluffs train, and at the depot stated to McHenry that had they taken his advice and settled in Kansas, they would be thousands of dollars better off.
November 6

-Alderman Kelly's well, down in West Kansas, was investigated yesterday, and at the bottom one or two dead rats were found. The water has had a peculiar taste for some time.
November 7

-Earthquake shocks were felt for the distance of one hundred and fifty miles west of this city, along the line of the Kansas Pacific Railway, yesterday morning. There were two distinct shocks. They were felt slightly in this city between four and six o'clock a.m.
November 9

-The skull of an infant was found by some small boys yesterday morning, while playing on the banks of the Kaw, near the Stock Yard water tank. Not knowing what it was, they proceeded to kick it about, and indulged in a lively game of football for a short time. At last, perceiving that it was a human head, they picked it up and carried it to the Stock

Yards, where it was handed over to Treasurer Richardson. Coroner Chew had best look into the matter.
November 11

-The steamboat Benton, which passed up the river about three months ago, passed down for St. Louis yesterday. She was as far up as Fort Benton, and returned with a load of furs.
November 12

-A couple of Chinamen, who were sufferers by the late destructive fire in Virginia City, arrived in this city yesterday morning and left their autographs on the register of the Barnum House. They are the advance guard of a party who propose locating in this city and starting a first class laundry.
November 12

-A horse was stolen from the public square night before last. The animal was hitched to a post just in the rear of the police station when made away with.
November 13

-The colored people of this city propose to start a paper, to be called the Western Enterprise, to be devoted to the interests of their people.
November 13

-Mark Twain's new sketches, just out, are meeting with rapid sale and a favorable reception in this city. It is a large, handsome volume of nearly four hundred pages, printed in clear, handsome type on heavy tinted paper, and is profusely illustrated with humorous engravings. The book is sold only by agents. Mr. W. F. Robinson is the agent for Kansas City. Those who admire Mark Twain's style and love a good hearty laugh will secure a volume of these sketches.

November 17

The title of this book is believed to be "Sketches Old and New".

-The following is the itemized rate of State and county taxation for the year 1875, the tax for which is now due and payable at the Collector's office at the court house: Rate on $100 is - State tax, 45c; county, 50c; special interest, 30c; poorhouse, 12½ c; bridge, 10c; Kansas City schools, $1; Kaw township Narrow Gauge Railroad, 25c; which makes a total of $2.72½ upon each $100.

November 25

-The human bones that had been excavated by grading the old cemetery on Oak street between Independence and Missouri avenues, and which had been boxed up and left upon the grounds, were yesterday taken in charge by the City Engineer and buried. The box in which they were placed had been split up and stolen for kindling wood. If there is any place where ghosts ought to walk, it is upon that desecrated piece of ground.

November 25

-Seventh street, between Walnut and Grand avenue, is being blasted out and widened.
December 5

-A reduction of car fare on the city railroads is contemplated. It is said that six tickets will be sold for twenty-five cents, instead of five, and that ten tickets to Westport can be bought for a dollar. This is a move in the right direction.
December 5

-The new elevator in West Kansas is getting so far up into the sky that it makes one dizzy-headed to look over its sides. The walls of the engine house, located just east of the building, are nearly up and ready for the roof.
December 16

-Evidences of the approaching holidays are apparent on every side. Toy and gift stores are prodigal in their showwindow displays, and the little ones are happy in anticipation of joys and toys to come. Evergreens for Christmas trees are also beginning to arrive.
December 16

-A TIMES reporter went up to the top of the new elevator yesterday afternoon, and, Oh! how the wind did blow. It is situated just in the right spot to get the full force of the winds from over towards Wyandotte, as they come whistling and rushing across the sandbars.
December 17

A Slice of the TIMES

-The old shell down in West Kansas, called a union depot, was packed full yesterday afternoon by travelers, coming and going by the different trains. Since the closing of the up-town ticket offices, the crowd about the West Kansas rookery, during train time, has increased wonderfully.
December 17

-St. Patrick's Church will be opened with appropriate services on Christmas day. Solemn high mass will be celebrated at half past ten o'clock, a.m., after which the opening sermon will be preached by Father Dalton, of the Church of Annunciation, West Kansas.
December 19

-The delinquent personal tax lists for 1875 have been turned over to Attorney Gibson for collection and due process of law. It's pay up or put up, now. The amount reported delinquent is $8,500.
December 21

-Last night the toy stores were thronged with people buying Christmas gifts for household pets.
December 25

-The stores throughout the city were crammed jam full all day long yesterday with holiday purchasers.
December 25

-Yesterday Mr. A. J. Kelly sent ten pounds of candies out to the Orphans Asylum, to be distributed among the forty waifs now lodged in that institution.
December 25

-Chief of Police Spears was made happy, yesterday, by some kind friend making him a present of a splendid turkey for his Christmas dinner.
December 25

-The residence of Frank Foster, Chief of the Fire Department, is now connected with the engine houses at the corner of Twelfth and Walnut streets and on Missouri avenue, by telegraph, and the alarm in case of fire can be given almost instantly.
December 29

"Why? Oh, why no registration?" - 1876

In 1876, the Nation turned 100 years old. Kansas City celebrated along with the rest of the country, although not as enthusiastically as in Philadelphia, where the great "Centennial Exposition" was held. All 38 states and many foreign countries had exhibits on the grounds and during the six months the Exposition was open to the public, attendance averaged around 274,000 per day.

The TIMES commemorated the Centennial with an unprecedented subscription drive. After installing their new Two Cylinder Hoe Press, and announcing that they were "now prepared to furnish any number of copies of the TIMES," the paper offered to the first 2,000 subscribers a "chance" in a drawing for dozens of "premiums." They increased their circulation substantially.

1876 was also a Presidential election year; one marred by the worst voting fraud the country had ever seen. The war against Chief Two Moons, Crazy Horse and Sitting Bull was well under way by spring and led to Custer's Last Stand in June. Many troop re-enforcements came through Kansas City headed west to fight. Alexander Graham Bell perfected and patented his invention, the telephone, and displayed it at the "Centennial Exposition". And a new gold rush had begun, this time in the Black Hills of South Dakota.

A Slice of the TIMES

A new building boom was underway by 1876, as Kansas City replaced many of her less adequate public buildings with better designed, better built new ones. New businesses were built and other businesses expanded, creating a larger work force and a shortage of housing. The one building Kansas City desperately needed to rebuild, the Union Depot, would have to wait another year.

1876 also marked the beginning of a twenty year legal battle between the city and the National Waterworks Company. Kansas City alleged the Waterworks Co. had not met the required specifications set out in their contract and, therefore, should not be paid. The National Waterworks Co. alleged that they had gone out of their way to meet the city's requirements, and even paid for land the city had promised to deed over to them.

In addition to all of this, James Pendergast moved down the river from St. Joseph to settle in Kansas City and took a job in the meat packing plants. Five years later, a well placed bet on a mare named Climax would start him on the road to becoming the most powerful man in Kansas City.

A Slice of the TIMES

-All the principal hotels in the city gave magnificent New Year's dinners to their guests. Some of their bills of fare were headed with a New Year's greeting.
January 2

-Gobblers were very scarce yesterday morning and many a family had to eat their dinner without the noble bird. Plankinton & Armour intended to give all of their employees a present of a turkey, but could not find enough in the market to go around.
January 2

-Patsey Dwyer, a brakeman on the Missouri River, Fort Scott & Gulf road, had his hand badly crushed, at Olathe, on Monday, while coupling cars.
January 6

-A test of Mr. Hall's safety car-coupler will be made on the Missouri River, Fort Scott & Gulf road, to-day.
January 6

-A couple of defunct canines floating in the pond on Grand avenue, between 16th and 17th streets, are eye-sores to the residents of that locality.
January 7

-Eighteen soldiers, black and white, arrived yesterday morning from Texas in charge of a lieutenant of the Tenth U.S. Infantry, and a squad of troops of that regiment. The eighteen were shackled

securely, and were being conveyed to Leavenworth, to serve out their terms of sentence in the military prison.
January 7

-According to the report of the County Assessor, property in Jackson county has increased in value $172,000 during the past year.
January 8

-Work on the new elevator is progressing so rapidly, that by the first of February it will be ready for the reception of grain. Men were engaged all day, yesterday, in hoisting the heavy machinery into position, and on Monday the smoke stack, 135 feet high, will be raised. The last of the tin roof was put on last night.
January 8

-The replacing of wooden street crossings with stone ones in different parts of the city is an improvement creditable to the present city government.
January 8

-A TIMES reporter was present yesterday when the prisoners in the county jail were given their dinner by Jailer Farrel. The meal consisted of good corn bread, pork-meat and potatoes and coffee. Every other day the prisoners are given soup. The men are fed in their cells, Farrel going along and opening the

doors and an assistant handing in the food. Among the noted characters now under surveillance are Blanchard, for robbing Mr. Neiswanger; Snarley, for the murder of McDonnell out near the fair grounds; McQuade, sentenced for two years to the penitentiary for perjury; Wagoner, sentenced for perjury; Never and Parmlee, the two young men corralled by Col. Coates, and last, but not least, "Rev." Gordon.
January 8

January 11, 1876, the Town Topics column was again renamed. This time it would be called Home News (but not for long!).

-The packing establishment of Plankinton & Armour, in West Kansas, is to be increased in size by the addition of a wing 200 feet long. On Christmas day three thousand and three hogs were slaughtered in the establishment, and yesterday, although it was a dull day, over one thousand were killed.
January 11

-Thirty-four hogs at an average weight of 587 lbs. were sold at the stock yards yesterday.
January 12

-Mormon Ann has been given 12 hours in which to leave the city. If found within the limits after that time she will be calaboosed.
January 12

-Something "legitimate" in the way of a female minstrel performance, the finale of which will be the gorgeous can-can, opens at the Opera House in this city to-night. The combination is known as "Madame Rentz's Great Original Female Minstrels", and embraces a "bower of fascinating beauty" said to be the most bewitching now on the road.
January 13

-If this cold weather holds on for a few days longer, the ice men of the city will begin the harvest. Last year the best cutting was on the 17th of January.
January 13

-Twenty-eight thousand dollars is the price the A., T., & S. Fe road paid the Kansas City Land company for eighteen acres of land in West Kansas.
January 13

-Over twenty-five hundred hogs were received at the Kansas Stock Yards yesterday. The day was a lively one among dealers, and prices ruled high. $6.00 per hundred was obtained for one lot.
January 13

-The interest in the union religious meetings, being held at Frank's Hall, continues to increase, and last night there were few if any vacant seats in the house. Large numbers of business men dropped in

A Slice of the TIMES

with their families and are helping the movement along by the influence of their presence; while some of them who are members of churches, take an active part in the evening exercises. An invitation is given each night for those who desire to change their course of life to manifest it by raising up or coming forward, and quite a number have already improved the opportunity and are continuing to do so each night. It is said that quite an awakening is also taking place in the different churches, and much good is resulting from these meetings.
January 14

-A car of fruit was yesterday received in this city from Boston, via St. Louis, K.C. & Northern road, which had been but seven days on the road.
January 15

-It would be a good idea if the Mayor would order out the water carts and have the streets sprinkled these terribly dusty days. Yesterday Main street was filled with clouds of the dirtiest kind of dust, and pedestrians had their eyes and mouths filled in anything but a pleasant manner.
January 15

-People were promenading the streets, yesterday, attired in summer habiliments, all oblivious to the fact that it was the 17th day of January.
January 18

"Why? Oh, why no registration?" - 1876

-People are probably not aware of the fact that 35 passenger trains leave the Union depot in this city every twenty-four hours.
January 18

-Tuesday night a big cock fight was indulged in at Atchison between the crack birds of that place and Leavenworth. Leavenworth's pit was rendered worthless at the first kick of the Atchison bird. Over $3,500 changed hands on the result.
January 20

-In about four or five weeks the citizens will have a chance to see how convenient a union depot at the State Line is. The outfit expect to occupy the old State Line House during the erection of the new depot.
January 26

-Ice cream will be fifty cents a dish next summer. This is reliable.
January 26

-Mr. D. N. Heizer, of Great Bend, Kansas passed through yesterday from the Eastern States, en route for home. Mr. Heizer is connected with the land department of the Atchison, Topeka & Santa Fe road. He states that the "Kansas Fever" is raging extensively throughout the North and East, and it is certain that there will be an immense tide of emigration this year to our sister State. That Kansas

is destined in the near future to be one of the most
populous and prosperous of the Western States, is a
fact that is plainly apparent.
January 27

-And still the warm weather continues.
January 28

-It is reported that ice is now housed up in Iowa
and Southern Nebraska 24 inches thick. If the report
is true, people in this vicinity need not weary about
a famine taking place next season.
January 28

-The old rag man has come to grief. His wagon
gave out before he did, and his song of rags, rags, is
suspended.
January 29

-The friends of a poor colored woman, who died on
Charlotte street last week, had a hard time keeping
the body for burial. It is said that a number of young
medical students attempted to steal the body and
take it to the dissecting room, and had it not been
for the timely arrival of a policeman, they would
have been successful. This is carrying matters a
little too far, and if such conduct is repeated, there
will be trouble.
February 2

-Whooping cough has removed quite a number of scholars from the primary department of Humboldt school, and the disease is quite prevalent in that neighborhood.
February 9

-A large number of people gathered together on the public square, near the market house, yesterday afternoon, to hear the law laid down by a disgusting looking man, who figured it out that the world was coming to an end in 1878. His harangue was listened to for over an hour. His features closely resembled a schoolboy's first attempt at the blackboard.
February 12

-Judge Sawyer, who has sent in his resignation, was first elected in 1871 and re-elected in 1874. His term of office would expire Jan. 1, 1880.
February 16

-The officer who arrested Abe Hickman for driving faster that the law allows over Bluff street bridge, failed to prove the charge, and Mr. H. was discharged.
February 16

-Mayor Gill was yesterday morning served with the papers in the water-works suit, by deputy U.S. Marshal Smith.
February 18

A Slice of the TIMES

-A number of emigrant wagons, bound for the Far West, passed through the city yesterday afternoon. Six prairie schooners were noticed on Main street at one time.
February 20

-Day before yesterday one of the biggest emigrant trains that ever passed through this city for Kansas, pulled out over the Atchison, Topeka & Santa Fe road. A special train, consisting of nineteen freight cars, loaded to the guards with horses, cows, hogs and sheep, farming tools, wagons and household goods of every variety, and also three passenger cars full of Illinoisans, with their families, came in over the North Missouri road and were transferred to the Santa Fe track. The party was under the leadership of Mr.   L. B. Hynes, the very efficient agent at St. Louis of the Atchison, Topeka & Santa Fe road. He was aided by Capt. R. M. Spivey, of the General Land Office of Topeka. The wide-awake freight agent here, Mr. E. H. Higgs, was on hand with a special engine and additional coaches, and he superintended the transfer at this point in his usual energetic and sympathetic style. On the arrival of the Missouri Pacific train, a car-load of emigrants (white) from Tennessee, en route to Great Bend, were assigned to a reserved coach on the Santa Fe train, and at midnight the long train of twenty-three freight and passenger cars went rumbling westward. The emigrants were ticketed to different places in the Arkansas valley, from Newton westward, and go

west well fixed to begin the work of preparing new homes. No more substantial and intelligent party of emigrants ever passed through our city than were those of that party. They are to be followed soon by many more from the district they have moved from.
February 20

-Col. C. C. Carpenter states that he has secured the services of Mr. John LaFebre, an old guide of Father DeSmet, as guide for his expedition in the Black Hills. This guide is positive he can lead the party to the spot spoken of by the Reverend Father where riches abound. The Colonel, when he arrives at the Black Hills, proposes to organize a company of 500 picked men and start for the place. It is in a locality that has never before been explored, only by a few trappers, and if half the guide tells is true, it is the richest mine in the world.
February 24

-Dennis Shire, for whipping one of his children, was placed in the cooler yesterday morning.
February 26

-One of Uncle Sam's letter carriers was dumped into a West Kansas muck hole, night before last, by an unruly horse.
February 26

-A mad dog created considerable excitement in West Kansas, Sunday afternoon. He was finally killed by a Mr. Darby.
February 29

A Slice of the TIMES

-Saturday the weather was as mild and pleasant as in May. Sunday it was as cold as December, and yesterday it was balmy and warm again.
February 29

-Good ice is being secured up in Nebraska by the ice men of this city.
March 1

-Mr. T. B. Bullene, versed as he is in many things, cannot remain on a horse's back when the saddle turns. Yesterday while slowly riding down Delaware street on a small sized pony, the sinch slipped and the well known dry goods man measured his length upon the ground.
March 1
Mr. Bullene was co-owner of "Bullene, Moore & Emery", one of the largest dry goods establishments in the area; the predecessor of "Emery, Byrd & Thayer".

-Seventeen car loads of 8-inch ice, direct from the Nemaha river, near Lincoln, Nebraska, were received in this city on Sunday last, by the K. C. & Wyandotte Ice Co. Superintendent Orbison is bound to have plenty of ice for next summer's use.
March 7

-Matt Clary, conductor on the Missouri River, Fort Scott & Gulf road, is the boy who makes it lively for evil doers. Yesterday on his train that left this city at 10:05 a.m. was a man dressed in woman's clothes. Matt had his eye on him from the moment

the train left this city. Near Olathe he collared the culprit and made him put down his false colors, and come out in his right dress. The man, underneath his dress, had a suit of grey Scoth clothes and looked like a respectable fellow. Why he wanted to travel in the attire of a female is one of those things no "fellah" can find out.
March 8

-There is a young man who roosts in a building on a public street who is in the habit of taking a bath in his wash-bowl, and then pitching his slop out the window. It's all right as long as the water freezes, but when warm weather comes about there is going to be trouble, if he doesn't cease. Yes, this is for you.
March 12

-Don't you forget it. This is for you: If you don't register to-day or to-morrow you can't come in on the election. And there will be no extension of time.
March 15

-These be hard times on the boys who swore off on the 1st. The candidates smile ever so nice, and almost force a man to put his mouth over a bottle.
March 15

-As an indication of the narrow-minded policy of the water works company, it need only be stated that although the TIMES pays the company for

using water to run its engine, it was compelled to pay extra for the few buckets full used in making mortar for the foundation of its new press. The water works company haven't got more friends than it needs already, and if run on the same principal for a few years longer it won't have any.
March 15

-Mercury crawled down to five degrees below zero yesterday.
March 18

-Yesterday was one of those days that made you feel as though you would like to meet your mother in-law and tell her what you thought.
March 18

-In wearing of the green, a man sometimes wakes up the morning after with a nose which reminds him of an Indian summer sunset, soft, red and mellow.
March 18

-Most positively, it is asserted, this is the last day to register. If you are a candidate you can do some good in drumming up the voters, if you never do any good any other way.
March 18

"Why? Oh, why no registration?" - 1876

-Herman, the great sleight of hand performer, is to appear at the Opera House three nights in April.
March 25

-Don't forget the eclipse of the sun to-day. The shadow will be best at about 3:30 o'clock. Get out your smoked glass, and don't get it out of a saloon either.
March 25

-There never was a municipal election before in this city when so much excitement was manifested as on yesterday. From early morn until 7 o'clock p.m. the streets were filled with excited individuals, and the whole city bore a holiday appearance.
April 5

-There was a lady at the polls in the Second Ward, yesterday, doing some tall electioneering. She carried no tickets, but called upon all to vote for temperance and purity. As there was no ticket in the field with those persons on it, her harangues were a failure. She carried a picture of George Washington, which she doubtless mistook for Twiss, and was trying to split the Gill faction.
April 5
Twiss and Gill were candidates for Mayor; Gill was running for re-election.

63

A Slice of the TIMES

-Defeated candidates might yesterday have been seen at almost any hour perambulating the back alleys and unfrequented streets while en route to their place of business.
April 6

-The entertainment by the renowned Herrmann at Turner Hall last night was attended by a good sized audience, and all were greatly pleased with what they saw - or rather, what they didn't see.
April 7

-The steamer Joe Kinney, so badly damaged during the late snow storm by coming in contact with the bridge pier of the Missouri river bridge, is being repaired at the dock opposite the old Gillis House.
April 7

-The world did not come to an end yesterday, notwithstanding the prediction of a certain class of fanatics.
April 9

-The splendid thick ice noticed yesterday, as it was being carted from the depot to the ice house, was shipped to this city from Minnesota.
April 9

-Crowds stopped at Bell's on Main street, and wondered what them red things were, and when informed that they were lobsters boiled in real sea

water they won't believe it. One old citizen remarked they must have been painted before leaving New York.
April 9

-The damages sustained by the steamer Joe Kinney, in passing through the draw bridge about two weeks ago, have been repaired and she left for St. Louis yesterday.
April 13

-Persons who do not like Kaw water can now have Missouri river water to their heart's content, as the "Big Muddy" has backed up to the pipes of the Waterworks Co. and the water is beautifully pellucid and clear (?).
April 15

-It is reported from a reliable source that during the present week ground will be broken for the new Live Stock Exchange building, at the Kansas Stock Yards. Forty thousand dollars is to be the cost, and it will be a highly ornamental structure, surpassing anything of the kind in the country.
April 16

On April 18, 1876, the TIMES changed the name of this column again, to City Summary; the last change until the 1890's.

-A corpse attired in black cloth clothing has been reported lying in a drift pile in the river, just below the city, for several days past. Wonder who he is.
April 18

-Open cars, with seats facing outwards a la Irish jaunting car, will soon be put on the street railway lines in this city. They are very very pleasant in summer time and will be
very popular.
April 19

-The patrons of the waterworks in West Kansas City are complaining that their water is very muddy. The trouble is, the Missouri is higher than the Kaw, and backs up beyond where water is taken from that river. They are getting Missouri water instead of Kaw water.
April 19

-Vast quantities of old bones pass through this city from the great plains every week. They are the last remains of the once magnificent herds of buffalo now almost extinct. These bones sell for ten dollars per ton, less than one half the price paid for them last year. They are sold in the East and ground up into fertilizers and bone dust for purifying and clarifying purposes. Dealers in these bones say the supply is almost inexhaustible.
April 19

-The plans for the new Cattle Exchange have been completed by the architect, A. J. Kelley, and have been accepted. The new building has been changed in its design since the issuance of the TIMES REVIEW. Ten thousand dollars' worth of improvements in the way of ornamentation have been added. It will have a Mansard roof and a verandah upon the eastern and southern fronts, and will be very tasty and handsome in its external appearance. The site for the new Exchange has been selected on the south side of the Stock Yards, on Sixteenth street and the State line. It will cost about $34,000.

April 23
The reporter is referring to the new Live Stock Exchange Building.

-The banks are receiving silver coin to exchange for fractional currency.

April 26

-Twenty cent coins are among the new silver currency. They come in handy in street car change or as change for any five cent purchase out of a quarter.

April 26

-Those who have saved samples of the fractional currency since the date of its first issue in 1862, will find their labor amply rewarded now. Paper shinplasters will soon be as scarce as hens' teeth, and in a few years a rare curiosity.

April 26

A Slice of the TIMES

-As an indication of the prevailing scarcity of ice, the following is submitted: J. H. McCoy of Joplin, has spent a few days in the city, endeavoring to purchase a few hundred tons for Joplin, and failed. He has gone to St. Louis to purchase. Ice in St. Louis is $15 and in Kansas City $20 per ton.
April 26

-The Germans met last night at Turner's Hall, to take action with reference to the proposed abolition of the German department and the High School grade in our public schools.
April 28

-Is this justice? The policeman who walks his beat all night and risks his life in defense of the public peace, receives $50 per month. The fireman who sleeps in his bed and attends a fire semi-occasionally, receives $60 per month. Is it right?
April 29

-A new stock yard is being built at the corner of Sixteenth and Grand Avenue by John Graydon. It will be a great convenience to the butchers and to the farmers who enter the city on the south side.
April 30

-The colored people held another meeting Thursday night to hear the report of the committee on the constitution for their proposed co-operative store, which was adopted. Their next move will be the election of officers, which takes place next

Thursday night, May 4th. Besides establishing a first class store, it is intended as so as the condition of the society will admit to put up their own building, to contain a fine hall for the use of its members and the public.
April 30

-The Joe Kinney consumed about one hour's time backing through the bridge yesterday. Steamboatmen are becoming very careful how they pass through bridges since the recent accidents here and in Hannibal.
May 5

-Twelfth street people are complaining bitterly at the treatment they have received at the hands of the city. They were obliged to pay their assessments for widening the street, a year ago, and the money collected from them has not been used for widening that street.
May 5

-Two of the new open-sided cars to be placed upon the Union Depot line, arrived yesterday. They are gay and light concerns. People will sit back and face outward.
May 7

-Corn cobs from the elevators are becoming quite popular as summer fuel.
May 10

A Slice of the TIMES

-The ice supply is far better than at first supposed. It can be had at $10 per ton.
May 10

-If you pay your taxes now, you get a rebate of 6 per cent. Pay up in May and save your money.
May 10

-A committee of twenty-one has been appointed to work up the grand Centennial Fourth of July celebration.
May 11

-Oh, my! won't the children be glad! The public schools close on the 31st of the present month and are not to open again till after the fall exposition. Lack of funds.
May 11

-It is startling but nevertheless true, that if Goodin's bill for the resurvey of the Kansas State line, which has passed its second reading, is adopted, all that portion of Kansas City west of Bluff street will be in Kansas.
May 13
Bluff Street was, and is, located just under the cliffs to the west of Quality Hill. If the State Line had been moved, all of the West Bottoms as well as points south would belong to Kansas.

-The contested election case in the Sixth Ward was brought up yesterday before the committee appointed to investigate. It was decided that the vote shall be recounted next Monday by the City Clerk and the committee, and the vote upon which was written "Murnett", instead of Burnett, shall be examined, and the person who cast it will be summoned to explain whether he did or did not intend to vote for Burnett.

May 13

The Sixth Ward was bounded by the river on the north, roughly Twelfth Street on the south, Pennsylvania Avenue on the east, and the State Line on the west.

-The Bottomites, or those residing in the Sixth Ward, are about to petition the City Council to give them a new election for alderman, and so settle the contested case between Burnett and Bigger. It is said that a re-examination of the ballots showed that there had been a number of illegal votes cast for all parties.

May 23

-"Vinegar Hill" is the popular name for all that portion of town south of 12th and west of Jefferson street.

May 28

-The grand jury ordered a half-dozen bottles of cologne to be sprinkled upon the foul smelling sawdust in their room.

May 28

A Slice of the TIMES

-Insects and mites now so numerous in cistern water may be killed by the use of a small quantity of lime thrown into the cistern.
May 28

-Now you get a rebate of the four per cent if you pay your taxes before the first of July.
June 1

-This is the first day of a very important month, politically. Both political parties nominate Presidential candidates.
June 1

-By all means have your cisterns cleaned out. Much of the sickness now so prevalent is caused by impurities washed from the roofs of houses.
June 1

-The interminable dispute as to who is Alderman in the Sixth Ward is still unsettled. It promises, however, to unseat both the present contestants and send the matter back to the people for settlement. Some three or four illegal votes have been thrown out on both sides.
June 1

-Boating on the placid, shady Kaw is becoming a favorite recreation Sunday afternoons.
June 6

-A catfish weighing about one hundred pounds was caught yesterday just above the waterworks reservoir. And still there are people who say there are no large fish in the Kaw.
June 6

-Talk about progress! One brick firm in this city has already sold twenty thousand bricks this season. Between eighty and ninety hands are employed making brick at this time.
June 6

-Two more street cars have been placed on the West Kansas City line to accommodate travel. The open side cars have been placed on the "belt line". People can now ride around the city from point to point for five cents.
June 6

-The people in McGee's addition objected to being summoned by the county to serve on juries, because they claim that it is not certain yet whether they live in Kansas or Missouri. The excuse is "too thin", at least that is what the Deputy Sheriff said as he yanked them along to court.
June 6

-Dr. Kellogg bought and fenced in the Walnut street spring. Now there are some people petitioning the Council for a portion of Kellogg's spring.
June 7

A Slice of the TIMES

-House rents are reported going up as houses become more difficult to find. There are few or no desirable houses for rent just now.
June 11

-The Sixth Ward contested election case will come up for final settlement tomorrow. By all means settle it one way or the other.
June 11

-The recent decision in the Sixth Ward appears to have pleased neither contestant.
June 15
Rather than hold another election, the City Council decided to let the "legal" votes stand, leaving Bigger the winner.

-The announcement that Col. Van Horn's prospects for the Republican Vice Presidential nomination were brightening created much comment in the city yesterday.
June 15
Col. Van Horn was, among many other things, the publisher of the TIMES' competition, the JOURNAL.

-The police are being called upon to enforce the ordinance prohibiting the erection of wooden awnings and posts on Main street. Merchants would avoid trouble and expense by using iron instead of wood.
June 15

"Why? Oh, why no registration?" - 1876

-The moral sensibilities of the good people of West Kansas City protest loudly against the base ball matches held near their churches and Sabbath Schools every Sunday. They propose to have the city ordinances enforced next Sunday by the police.
June 16

-A very handsome ornamented floor of white ash and walnut is being laid in Gardner's billiard hall. It is the handsomest and costliest floor in the West.
June 16

-A steamboat for the Black Hills is expected to arrive here on Monday. The proprietors are carrying passengers through from Kansas City to Rapid or Custer City via Brule City for $15 each. Scalps not insured.
June 17

-Louis Thoman, the young man who stole ten head of cattle from J. B. Wornall's pasture, a few weeks ago, and sold them to Kansas City butchers, was sentenced yesterday to three years in the Penitentiary.
June 17

-A poor, lost creature named Delia Graves attempted to shuffle off this existence by a dose of morphine, on Saturday night. Officer McCarty and Dr. Lewis saved her life. Why cannot such people be let alone when they desire to shake off a life of sin, shame and misery?
June 20

-George Hale is introducing his patent horse-hitching apparatus into the St. Louis Fire Department. Sweet & Butler are getting up some of the machinery.
June 23

-The Freedman's Record is the title of a new paper just started by Messrs. H. R. Graham and R. W. Foster. It is published by colored people in the interest of the African race. The first number is a bright, interesting sheet, moral in sentiment, candid and moderate in politics, and filled with well-prepared original reading. The TIMES welcomes the Record, and wishes it every success.
June 24

-An excursion up the river is spoken of for the Fourth of July.
July 2

-The Buckner Band is the bulliest band in the county. All the members play on cow bells.
July 2

-Thirty car-loads of coal were sold here yesterday at less than ten cents per bushel. McKinley made the sale. Coal is getting cheap.
July 2

-The city has at last discovered that the $2,500 worth of railroad ties purchased for the Santa Fe switch have been stolen. No one is responsible of course.
July 2

-The Twelfth street widening muddle seems to be as far from adjustment as ever. It is the city this time and not the property owners which is delinquent.
July 2

-The bonds of the new Union Depot Company have been placed on deposit in St. Louis, and work will be commenced as soon as a sale has been effected. That is cheering.
July 8

-Sam Polowasky, a junk shop keeper, has been selling whisky to the colored population at five cents per drink. He was brought to his happy home - the calaboose - for a violation of the license ordinance, was fined $80, and appealed his case. Polowasky is a bad egg.
July 8

-It is a good sign to see the engineers of the new Union Depot settling down to business and taking measurements for the new building.
July 9

A Slice of the TIMES

-The Indian war is the principal topic of conversation just now.
July 12

-The ice monopoly is being badly broken up by outside competition. A man from Lawrence has 250,000 pounds on the market at 65 cts., and there is a prospect of ice coming down to 50 cents. And still the war goes on.
July 12

-Why cannot the poor, afflicted public who use the Union Depot shed have water to drink. Yesterday the water in the tank was warm and filthy and ladies and children were obliged to go out to saloons to seek water. Whose fault is it that no good water is ever found in the Union Depot?
July 12

-It is said that no more licenses will be issued to saloon keepers in the block between Fifth, Main and Missouri avenue. That will drive saloon keepers into new quarters.
July 13

-It will be satisfactory for some people to know that the "flexible" India rubber stuffed club is coming into fashion. The Kansas City police will soon be armed with them.
July 15

-Cole Younger visited some of his friends in Lee's Summit on Sunday night. He was splendidly mounted and well dressed. Tuesday evening he enjoyed an evening with Tony Pastor, in company with one or two of his city cousins.
July 27

-Wife beating is becoming very popular just now in this city, much to the disgrace of the masculine portion of the community. A great six foot athlete named Martin Cavanaugh, living on the hill west of Turner Hall, was caught beating the floor with the body of his little weeping wife. He was very properly sent to jail to meditate upon his debasement, and await trial. Yesterday morning he paid $25 as the penalty for his cruelty.
July 27

-The funeral of old Mrs. Chick, the mother of some of the founders of this city, was attended largely by the friends of that much respected family. Mrs. Chick, since the departure of Madame Chouteau was entitled to the honor of being the mother of this city. Her memory will live green for generations to come.
July 27

-The old shed - misnamed "Union Depot" - is being ventilated. Eight or ten windows are being put into it to give the outraged public a chance to breathe, and to give the poor emigrant daylight in

which to pick off their tormentors. The old shed has become too filthy with vermin for clean people to trust their garments with it.
July 28

-Yesterday morning when Mr. Henry Bedgood opened his store on Fourth street he found Wm. Patterson, who generally opens the store, absent. On going to his room in the brick building on the corner of Fourth and Walnut streets, Patterson and his family were found asleep and almost stupefied from the effects of chloroform. The room had been entered in the night, and about $100 taken from under Patterson's head. No clue to the thieves was discovered.
July 29

-The detectives who have been working up the cause of the breaking of the large $600 pane of glass in Bullene, Moore & Emery's front window, have found out the breaker. It turns out to be a boy who threw a stone at Joe Bleach's dog. The stone missed the dog, glanced from the pavement, and struck the window. One or two discharged employees had been suspected.
August 3

-Coal dealers speak of an inevitable reduction of coal during the coming fall and winter. The opening of new coal banks at Montserret, on the Missouri Pacific, the enlargement of the Huntsville mines, on

the North Missouri, and the opening of the Narrow Gauge to Lexington will give a lively competition. Coal is sold here by the car load now at 9 ½ c, which is a great reduction from 16c and 18c, the old prices.
August 3

-The annexation of Kansas City to Kansas is once more a topic of discussion since the resurvey of the State line has been brought before Congress.
August 4

-Yesterday afternoon a lady driving up Main street with two gray horses, while attempting to pass a number of teams in front of Smith's saloon, between 8th and 9th, ran the hub of the buggy wheel against one of the posts supporting the awning and it being in a fair condition to tumble, just gave one lunge and came down. Result, one less "old wood awning."
August 5

-A weather-bronzed mountaineer, attired in buckskin from head to the sole of his feet, attracted some attention in the Depot last evening. It was his first visit to the "States" in twelve years. He wore an old belt with the letters "C.S.A." on the buckle.
August 8

-A party of 590 Mennonites, including men, women and children, passed through the city yesterday, on their way to Hays City, Kansas, on the

A Slice of the TIMES

Kansas Pacific Railroad. Mr. Roedelheimer, the Land Agent of the Company, had charge of the party. This makes 1,400 Mennonites that he has escorted through here in the last two weeks. Come on, Roedelheimer, with your "Men on nights," and days, they will be a fine addition to Kansas, and will do their trading in Kansas City.
August 9

-A party of three well armed horse thief hunters rode into town yesterday, each with a supply of rope on his saddle. They refreshed themselves and started on a hot trail eastward. A hanging item may be expected to day.
August 9

-The proposed new sewer in West Kansas City will be the largest sewer in the city. It will be one large stone sewer reaching from the Missouri river across the bottoms, with branches extending on each side of it where drainage is required.
August 10

-Live stock business being dull yesterday two prominent stock men took to trading their old clothes. Fits were not guaranteed and the least man looked like an advertisement for a bag factory.
August 11

-The Ghost on the levee and in the vicinity of the New Court House raised quite an excitement last night. Why don't the police either banish the

horrible looking apparition or capture it? If two officers can't capture it send four. It is getting to be a nuisance.
August 11

-A letter was shown to Billy Gardner yesterday from Jim Vivian, an old miner who is in the Black Hills. Vivian says the boys are making from $10 to $50 a day right along, and new discoveries being made all the time.
August 13

-Music, water spray and good company were the accompaniments at the Vienna Garden last evening. Prof. Banmaster played his medley, much to the amusement of the pleasure seekers. Mr. Caro exerted himself to make it pleasant for his guests, and succeeded satisfactorily.
August 13

-Wild Bill, the long-haired gentleman of leisure, who loafed about this city for so long, is reported killed in the Black Hills mines. He married Madame Lake, the circus rider, last winter in Cheyenne, and has been shot by the brother of a man he killed in Abilene, Kansas, years ago. Retribution.
August 13

-Alderman Holmes introduced an ordinance yesterday to establish and put in force the so called "Sunday law." It was read and referred to the

ordinance committee. The ordinance prohibits all kinds of labor or business on Sunday.
August 15

-The flags were at half-mast yesterday in respect to ex-Mayor Lykins.
August 17

-Two companies of the 11th Infantry came in last night from Fort Brown, Texas, and left on the Council Bluffs road for Fort Benton. They go to help Gen. Terry to fight Sitting Bull. They were all sorry they could not attend tonight's meeting.
August 18

-The bloody Sixth Ward, with such men as Burnett, Kelly, Kirby, O'Rourke, Cunningham, will not forget the opening of the campaign to-night, at Turner Hall. Come up, boys.
August 18

-For renting his rooms to a frail female called "Big Jenny," D. Loeb was fined $29.25. But why was Loeb made an exception? There are rooms along Main street full of the soiled doves.
August 20

-George Washington is again in trouble. Last time he was arrested for beating Martha Washington, his wife. Now he is in jail charged with stealing six hogs, valued at sixty dollars. He ought to have his name changed.
August 24

"Why? Oh, why no registration?" - 1876

-To Jesse James. A package was received at this office, last night, from Baron Montgomery, addressed to "Jesse James, Safe Retreat, care Kansas City TIMES." The package and letter will be delivered to any known person, on application to the "local" of this paper.
August 25

-Two companies of the Eleventh Infantry - about thirty to a company - passed through from Texas last evening on their way to reinforce Crook. Sixty men, forty fit for duty, and ten able to hit a barn door at thirty paces. Nice men to meet Indians, who can hit a nine spot at fifty yards at a full gallop! More men for Sitting Bull.
August 25

-The market yesterday morning was the largest of the season, the wagons extending entirely around the Market House and up to Main on 4th, and half way across the square south from the building. Everything, from a shelled bean to a whole ox, was temptingly displayed and from the number of purchasers one would judge "marketing" was financially lively. Many strangers were noticed looking in and around the busy scene commenting on the Western way of doing biz.
August 27

-A raid was made last night on a den of prostitution on Fifth street, near the Little Broadway. A little

fourteen year old girl named Low Martin was taken with the woman of the house. She said she had been seduced from her home near Richmond, Ray county, and brought to Kansas City and deserted by her betrayer. She will be sent to her parents. Ida Faxton and the other woman in the house were sent to jail.
September 2

-The old depot shed was washed out yesterday morning, and the swarms of creeping vermin driven from the floor to the seats. There is only one way to cleanse the old barn, and that is to burn it or pull it down.
September 2

-A contemporary gets off the following, suggested by a scene at the Union Depot yesterday morning:

Thinking of wife and home,
    The weary traveler sits
Upon the depot seats,
    And picks.
        And picks.

What would SHE say,
    His fond, expectant spouse,
To see him sitting there
    To swear,
        And "louse."
September 2

-The police change their beats once in two months. This is for the information of those who are unaccustomed to strange faces on their nocturnal rambles after false idols.
September 6

-The primp, pretty school marms put on an extra primp and walk down Main street as the nearest way to school these mornings. Their bustles have just the nicest possible poise as they trip daintily on their way to school.
September 6

-A vote was taken on the Narrow Gauge train yesterday. 19 for Tilden, 13 for Hayes.
September 17

-It is intended that on next Thursday the corner stone of the new Exchange building will be laid with imposing Masonic ceremonies.
September 17

-To-morrow the next great Exposition of Kansas City will open. It is sure to be a big success every way. There will large crowds come from abroad, many of whom will stay all the week.
September 17

-The Chief of Police desires to warn the citizens to be cautious about leaving their houses unguarded this week. Instead of an entire family going to the

Fair, some one had better remain to see that the house is not entered by sneak thieves, who already are flocking to this city in large numbers.
September 19

-Fifteen beeves, one hundred and twenty sheep, twenty five hogs, and five car loads of turkeys and chickens have been provided for to-morrow's barbecue on the Exposition grounds. Everybody invited.
October 11

-H. C. Crenshaw has just completed the finest and most complete horse and mule market in the West. It is on Fifth Street, in the rear of the new Merchant's Exchange. It is the largest and best stable now in Kansas City.
October 12

-Whew! But that old depot shed is loud. The stench emanating from the closets upon the sidewalks is sufficient to create sickness. Why does the health officer neglect his duty.
October 14

-Coal is selling at 16 cents, and a limited supply in the market.
October 15

-Work will be commenced on Monday on the great sewer to be built through West Kansas City. It will reach from Twelfth street to the Missouri River, and

if the weather proves favorable will be completed before the spring rains arrive. Mr. John Halpin has the contract. The sewer will cost about $25,000.
October 15

-Yesterday afternoon about 2 o'clock a horse attached to a light vehicle broke away from Briggs' blacksmith shop, on Broadway and Fifth streets. The animal dashed at full speed up Fourth to Delaware street, where it turned and ran upon the pavement in front of the Pacific House Saloon. There it fell upon its side, the force of the fall forcing its legs and head into a window or ventilator beneath the door. There it lay powerless, amid a pile of harness, wheels and the other wreck of the outfit. The owner, a Mr. Howell, came up just as the horse was rescued. The animal, a very fine one, was not seriously injured.
October 18

-Let us register.
October 19
-Have you registered?
October 19

-When is the election?
October 19

-No one knows when.
October 19

-Why! Oh, why no registration?
October 19

A Slice of the TIMES

-Less than three weeks to the Presidential election, and no campaign preparations noticeable in this vicinity.
October 20

-Good mechanics are in demand; poor ones are plenty. Still every man who will work experiences no difficulty in obtaining a job.
October 20

-The brickmakers are working night and day in anticipation of cold weather. The demand for brick has not been so good for five years past.
October 20

-A vote taken yesterday afternoon among the stock men in the Kansas Stock Yards resulted as follows: Tilden, 47; Hayes, 7. This is one of the best political straws of the season.
October 20

-George Hale has sold a half interest in his new rotary engine. A new six horse-power engine will be made at once with new improvements and the engine will then be manufactured to order as fast as required.
October 25

-Measles have become an epidemic in the southern half of the city.
October 25

"Why? Oh, why no registration?" - 1876

-The receipts of cattle at the Kansas City stock yards during the past week have been 12,500 head.
October 25

-The Academy of Science in their labors last Sunday, in the mounds on the bluffs opposite this city, discovered eight or ten skeletons. They are supposed to be the remains of a race of men who occupied this country long before the arrival of the Indians in this land. The bones are gigantic in size and were all found in a sitting posture in a rude stone tomb, or sarcophagus.
November 2

-The betting on the election results is becoming interesting. An enterprising Yankee came in last evening and set up a pool selling "masheen" in one of the fashionable saloons. You can pay in your "stamps" and take your choice, either on the general result or any State in the Union - all for the small sum of five dollars.
November 2

-The Union Depot shed is to be repaired at once for winter use.
November 3

-The plastering is finished on the new Stock Exchange building. What remains to be done is the inside woodwork, such as casings, etc., and painting, which will take most of this month to complete.
November 3

A Slice of the TIMES

-The excavation for the big sewer in the Bottoms is full of water, with no outlet. Work will have to be delayed until it dries out or is pumped out or drained.
November 3

-If any one knows who are the judges of election for Kansas City, or where the voting will take place next Tuesday, they will confer a favor by notifying the city editor of this paper. No public notification either of judges or places of election has yet been made.
November 5

-Vote early.
November 7

-No registration required.
November 7

-Kansas City "went on a tear" yesterday.
November 9

-Pay your bets.
November 9

-The best bet made on the election is that between Messrs. Shough and Campbell, live stock men of this city. They each agree that the loser of the bet shall ride in the dead cart of the Kansas Stock Yards through the streets of this city, attired in a calico

dress and wearing horns; and that the stock dealers will walk behind in procession.
November 10

-The Presidential excitement is paralyzing business of every description.
November 14
Although the election had taken place a full seven days earlier, the final results were not known. Tilden had taken Missouri (as well as Kansas City) by a vast majority, but the rest of the union was split. Louisiana, South Carolina and Florida were still to close to call.

-Fine fresh venison sells at 8c per lb. and prime roasts of beef or beefsteak and pork sausage at the same price at the packing house. This is a blessing the people of Kansas City do not fully appreciate.
November 17

-Election result is in a fog.
November 18

-Those who bet wish they had not.
November 18
In fact, it would be several weeks before the "general result" was know, prompting many gamblers to demand that interest be paid on their held moneys.

-The new Live Stock Exchange is to be opened in a formal manner in a few days.
November 18

A Slice of the TIMES

-A movement is about to be made to secure an enlargement or improvement of the city market house. It is too small for the amount of business transacted in it, and experience has shown that it is the most profitable public institution in the city. It is more than self-sustaining, but in its present miserable condition it is a nuisance.
November 19

-The Waterworks suit will go on until next May, when it will be decided whether the Waterworks Company has complied with its contract or not.
November 26

-A grand Thanksgiving dinner was given on Thursday by Mrs. Barnum to the friends of Barnum. The bill of fare was one of the best ever produced in this city. It is so long that a man would get hungry to read it through. Mrs. Barnum is determined to keep up the reputation of her most excellent house.
December 2

-A case of abortion was reported at police headquarters about one o'clock this morning. The girl is an inmate of Julia Sweet's establishment, on Commercial alley, and was reported dying. The case promises to be somewhat interesting as there is a physician in it.
December 3

-The prisoners in the jail complain bitterly of the food and bedding furnished them. A reporter who examined the cells of the prisoners last evening would remark that the condition of the jail beneath the new court house is at this time a scandal to civilization. In one dark iron box three man are confined, with no bed and only one blanket. In another two men have only one narrow mattress and a blanket. The prisoners were howling for food and shivering from cold. Marshal Ligget has made preparations for the prisoners relief.
December 8

-The drag-net was hauled through the gambling houses last night and about twenty men "pulled" to the Police Court. All gave bonds for appearance this morning, when they will pay $14 each or go to the workhouse. All kinds of men were caught in the haul - farmers, dry goods clerks, merchants, butchers, frontiersmen, boys, loafers, pimps, and the usual assortment of professional gamblers.
December 12

-Prof. Tice will deliver a course of three lectures at Coates' Opera House on the 10th, 11th and 12th of January. Everybody will want to hear what the "clerk of the weather" has to say for himself.
December 16
Professor Tice was the State's often quoted and reasonably reliable weatherman. He lived in St. Louis and reported to the cities via the telegraph.

95

A Slice of the TIMES

-The new Live Stock Exchange will be appropriately dedicated to-morrow by the live stock men and their friends.
December 24

-Among the Christmas presents made yesterday was a handsome oil painting, a portrait of Col. R. T. Van Horn, which was presented to Mr. Aleck Lacy, the city editor of the Journal. The present was a very appropriate one and, will be fully appreciated by Mr. Lacy, who is a great admirer of his editor-in-chief. The name of the gentleman making the present was not obtainable.
December 25

-The city presented a very gay appearance all day Monday. A few sleighs were out with the sparsely falling snow, and gave a romantic look to the city that has been lacking for some time. Sorry Christmas don't come oftener.
December 26

-There was a grand chicken fight on Christmas night in the pit on the corner of Sixteenth and Grand avenue. A lot of fine birds were brought over from Liberty, Clay county. The fighting was kept up all night. Thirteen birds were killed in the battle. More than forty battles were fought. A challenge has been sent to Leavenworth breeders to bring on their chickens. It is a queer pastime, but then it is fun for the boys.
December 28

96

The Brickmakers Harvest
1877

The Presidential Election of 1876 had been, to put it mildly, a mess. Although Tilden, the Democratic candidate, was ahead by as many as 264,000 votes, he still needed one electoral vote to win. It appeared that the states of Florida, South Carolina, Louisiana and Oregon had used intimidation or other illegal practices in providing Democratic majorities, and a special commission of 15, eight Republicans and seven Democrats, was organized to review the votes. Their decision followed party lines and the Senate President announced the election of Rutherford B. Hays on March 2, 1877. He was sworn in as President three days later. For people unhappy with the decision, he would be known as President "Rutherfraud" thereafter.

Also in 1877, Thomas A. Edison patented his phonograph. The invention played cylinders made of tin rotating on a drum spun by a hand crank. Although the instrument was primitive compared to his later wax cylinder machines, the sound quality was quite good. Edison never envisioned his machine would become popular for musical purposes, but rather expected it to be used to record speeches. Hence the name, "Talking Machine."

In Kansas City, the newly realized building boom was taking almost everyone by surprise. The TIMES began printing a daily list of the city's Building Permits in an effort to keep track of the new developments. The greatest strain, however, was felt by the brickmakers. New kilns were opened and by late April, 75,000 bricks a day were being made. But it was still not enough.

97

A Slice of the TIMES

-Ice is now only 90 cents per ton.
January 1

-Who has written 1876 for 1877?
January 3

-The W. U. Telegraph Company has recently perfected arrangements so that messages can be sent from their offices at the Live Stock Exchange, Grain Board and up town, direct to Chicago, without repeating at St. Louis, as has heretofore been the case.
January 9

-Doc. Henderson is a gentleman of color. He was taken in on Sunday afternoon while vigorously engaged in supporting a lamp post in the classic locality of Third and Grand avenue. He was very obstreperous. While in the police office he tore one of the officer's Sunday pants, and asserted that the decent of another could be traced to canine origin. Not having the lucre he went to the workhouse.
January 9

-Neiswanger Bros. have just received a lot of very handsome new sleighs. They are just in time for the sleighing season.
January 10

The Brickmaker's Harvest - 1877

-An attractive feature in West Kansas City just now is the Automatic Museum, fitted by George Gooch, at the broad gauge. It consists of a full musical orchestra run by clockwork, a negro preacher, two acrobats performing on a bar, negro clog dancers, two tight rope performers, a train of cars running at full speed around a landscape, a string band formed by four trained cats and several other curiosities. When these figures are set in motion it forms a very curious scene. Gooch is general manager and Toms the proprietor of the queer collection.
January 10

-A party of young people got upset and sadly spilled out into the snow out near Westport Tuesday night. There is lots of fun when you go sleighing.
January 11

-The ferryboat Pomeroy, which has been tied up on the opposite side of the river, has been brought to this side through a channel cut in the ice. It was a hard task, but will save the boat from the fate of the steamer Lizzie, which went down in the ice gorge several years ago.
January 13

-A mammoth sleigh, containing upwards of twenty persons, and drawn by four horses, made a good showing on Main
January 13

A Slice of the TIMES

-There were twenty persons sleeping on the floor around the stove in the old Recorder's Court room last night. Some supported their heads on pillows of stove wood; some need their coats, and one colored person's head was in the empty coal bucket.
January 13

-Plenty of snow and no school yesterday, consequently the boys indulged extensively in coasting.
January 14
"Coasting" was the term for sledding, although a sled was not always used.

-At dark last night every nice sleigh in the city had been engaged for Sunday.
January 14

-Five dollars per hour for a sleigh ride is rather steep, but the boys must have some of it even at that price.
January 14

-A new ordinance, approved by the Mayor on Wednesday, prohibits the burial of any person within the city limits.
January 19
All cemeteries, with the exception of the old City Cemetery, were located outside the city limits anyway.

-A drunken fool created some little stir in the Union Depot yesterday by exhibiting a package containing $500, which he had received from the sale of some hogs. He was warned by the police that a gang of sharpers were dogging his steps, but he laughed at his danger. It will be a wonder if he gets home to Junction City without being robbed.
January 20

-The women who are known as keepers of houses of bad reputation in this city were fined yesterday the usual amount, $29 each. This is nothing more nor less than a license, although not called by that name. It is better, however, than the old mode of public raids, wherein the women were driven to the police office in droves like so many sheep.
January 20

-Over two hundred and twenty thousand bushels of corn were sold yesterday at the grain board, the bulk of which was for March delivery. This is the heaviest day's transaction since the board was established, less than six months ago.
January 23

-Another coasting casualty. A little boy, nine years old, broke his arm while coasting on the east side of town yesterday. This is one among a dozen similar cases which have happened within a past.
January 23

-People now cross over the river on the ice with loaded teams. The wood dealers are taking advantage of the opportunity to import large quantities of cordwood.
January 25

-The ice in the Missouri River at this point is in a decomposed condition. Parties crossing over it with teams are liable to be left at any minute.
February 1

-The Black Hills fever is breaking out all over the city. Several of the leading young men of Kansas City are preparing to start for the land of Gold. Kansas City will be well represented in the hills this year.
February 3

-Prof. R. H. Moore is going to put down an ash floor in McDowell's Hall and introduce parlor skating. He has made arrangements for the opening soon.
February 4

-The total debt of Kansas City is $1,467,795.
February 4

-The Auditor reports $76,631 in city greenbacks in circulation.
February 4

The Brickmaker's Harvest - 1877

-There are between eighty and ninety saloons licensed in this city.

February 4

-The Council has at last resolved to take action on the subject of doors. It proposes to legislate so that doors to all public places shall be made to open outwardly.

February 6

This legislation was the result of public outcry after a theater fire in New York the previous year. People franticly trying to escape the blaze were crushed against doors that opened inward.

-The ferryboat, S. C. Pomeroy, was carried away from her moorings by the ice gorge which came down the river on Monday night. She is now helplessly blocked in a park of ice opposite the north end of Walnut street. Steam is kept up constantly, and it is thought that the boat will succeed in getting out of the scrape.

February 7

-Plows, drills, cultivators, horse hoes, corn planters, and various other implements of husbandry of every conceivable pattern, manufacture and design are now arriving in the city, car load after car load. Agricultural implement dealers are busy "from early morn till dewy eve" receiving and storing them away for spring trade, thus giving employment to numbers of willing hands, who are doubtless mighty glad of a job.

February 7

A Slice of the TIMES

-If you see quite a number of people to-day who
are pretty badly "bunged up," don't too hastily jump
to the conclusion that they have been in a free fight
- it was only a severe case of roller skating.
February 10

-Walter Wilson, on his weaving
   Way down Main street, went believing
   That he wouldn't be arrested,
   Nor while on his spree molested,
   'Twas'nt water made him totter,
   No, indeed, for he had got a
   Half a dozen five cent whiskies
   In his stomach, and did risk his
   Precious life that poison drinking,
   And he reeled on, little thinking
   He would be right promptly landed
   In the jug - and yet be candid
   Truth is, Walter did fetch up there,
   Dined there, yes, and he did sup there.
   And when came the rosy morning,
   With the briefest kind of warning
   He was brought before the Recorder,
   Charged with drunkenness and disorder
   Ly proceedings, and was sent out
   To the workhouse, and went out,
   Though protesting, with great clamor,
   He would never wield a hammer
   On the rock pile of the city;
   But he *will*. So ends this ditty.
February 14

104

The Brickmaker's Harvest - 1877

-The rush for valentines yesterday was unprecedented in this city. Harry Wright was obliged to keep the post office store open until a late hour to accommodate the demand.
February 15

-McDowell's Hall now presents a smooth, glassy floor, either for roller skating or dancing, and is appreciated by all who participate in either. Prof. Moore gave a social hop last evening and to-night the hall will be open for roller skating.
February 15

-A census taken last year by Father Dalton, in his parish, showed a decrease of nearly 50 families, most of whom had gone to California. This years census shows an increase of about 150 families, or 100 more families than there were in West Kansas one year ago.
February 15

-George Hale, the young man who has just succeeded in perfecting a patent rotary engine, yesterday completed a twelve horse power machine at the Keystone works. His invention promises to be a revolution in steam power machinery. Mr. Hale is a member of the Fire Department, and has devoted several years to perfecting his machine.
February 17

A Slice of the TIMES

-Big complaints of dead dogs in the Bottom. Five on St. Louis avenue and fifteen or twenty between the Live Stock Exchange and Twelfth street, besides about a hundred and one scattered around at other points. Better that the curs be dead than alive, but better still that they be put under ground.
February 22

-A petition is being circulated to have a gas lamp lighted upon Main street between the levee and Second street. This is nothing but right. Broadway has gas lamps on both sides; why not Main street, which has far more traffic, be allowed one lamp between the river and the Court House?
February 25

-The Academy of Science met last night in the rooms of the Y.M.C.A. to listen to a report of Judge West on the Clay county mound exhumations.
February 28

-Yesterday afternoon about half-past three the alarm of fire from the Second Ward was sounded, drawing a large crowd to the corner of Seventh and Delaware, it proving to be a shanty occupied by two colored families. The engines were soon at work, but the building was a total wreck, and what the fire did not damage the water did. While the engines were at work the hose burst and deluged the spectators, to the delight of those escaping. The origin of the fire was a defective flue.
February 28

106

-Now that the Presidential fraud has been consummated, the people are all turning their attention to something more interesting than politics. The change of topic of conversation will be a welcome one to everyone.
March 3
The Inauguration took place on March 5.

-On and after to-day, the Western Union Telegraph rates to New York, Philadelphia, Baltimore, Boston, Cincinnati, Toledo, and all other large eastern points will be reduced to 50c. Half rate messages of twenty words will be accepted for the same places.
March 13

-Wm. Winner, the very popular and efficient Assistant Postmaster of this city, will vacate his present position on the 1st of April, and will go into the newspaper advertising and subscription agency.
March 24

-The ferry-boat S. C. Pomeroy sprung a leak and sunk during the hurricane Friday night. She will prove a total loss.
March 25

-The heaviest shipment of dried buffalo ever received in Kansas City was placed in the warehouse of Dorseif & Ortloff yesterday, over forty thousand pounds.
March 30

A Slice of the TIMES

-Now for the millennium! A Republican President, a Republican Mayor and a Republican City Council.
April 5

-The rear portion of a house on Third street, between Walnut and Grand avenue, fell Thursday night. No one was injured.
April 7

-Real estate men report rents on the ascendancy. Houses which formerly rented for twenty-five dollars per month are now in demand at thirty-five and forty dollars. They are scarce even at those figures.
April 7

-The steamer Joe Kinney and barge, which arrived at St. Louis Thursday, is said to have carried the largest cargo ever taken out of the Missouri river. She had 1,000 tons of produce, one item of which was 14,124 sacks of grain. A portion of her freight was taken on at this point, which is fast gaining a world-wide reputation as a commercial mart.
April 7

-The time is fast coming when the dog which can not sport a registration tab will be consigned to the tender mercies of dog-catchers, and from thence to the sausage manufacturer, from whence he will issue ready to grace the table of the boarding house keeper.
April 8

-Radishes sell for a cent apiece in the Market House.
April 8

-A bran new side-wheel boat will soon enter the trade between here and St. Louis. She is called the Gold Dust.
April 8

-The levee, yesterday, was the scene of busy activity, and for a time regained its air of importance as of old. There was a more than usual movement among the boats; four arrivals and three departures being observed.
April 12

-A newly invented process is being introduced for steaming beer in bottles. Spengler & Brother have just had a large tank prepared in which bottled beer is placed and heated. After undergoing this process beer can be transported to Mexico or any other distant region.
April 15

-The new sewer being built by Contractor Halpin was badly damaged by the rain. A portion of the new work, built upon a loose sand foundation, is reported caved in on Santa Fe street. The damage is said to be quite serious.
April 19

A Slice of the TIMES

-The terms of Chief Police Speers and Captain Dennis Malloy will expire to-morrow. They were appointed for a term of three years, and having general satisfaction there is no intention upon the part of the Commissioners to make a change. Applicants for these positions may take the hint.
April 19

-The Union Depot question is beginning to assume something like a tangible shape. By reference to the advertising columns of the TIMES this morning it will be seen that the order of publication for the condemnation of the necessary ground, so as to complete the title thereof, is being made. The bonds have been negotiated and positive assurances are given that work will be commenced very soon.
April 19

-Dornseif & Ortloff's ice house is now the property of the Sheridan pond. They propose a suit against the city, as their ice crop is gone. The heavy rains took it in.
April 21

-There will be a boat race this evening on the Laclede Lake, opposite the Union depot. The two boats will start at 5 o'clock. Fifty dollars a side is the stakes.
April 21

-The Western Review of Science and Industry for the month of April, is out. It is a number replete with useful and interesting information, and is worth ten times the purchase price. It contains chapters on archaeology, Geography, chemistry, astronomy, natural history, scientific miscellany and editorial notes, by its talented editor, Theodore S. Case.
April 21

-The "Riverview Park" is the name of the new race track near the Live Stock Exchange. A fine horse barn has been added to the attractions of the course, and Mr. A. D. Carson, the Superintendent, late from Brighton Mass., has charge of these stables.
April 24

-Chiquita and Lady Veto, the two Kansas City favorite racers, were out on the new mile track near the Stock Yards yesterday. Col. Wm. Mulkey will start his two pets eastward next week.
April 24

-Colonel Kersey Coates has been having an interesting time during the past two days clearing the "patch" of shanties on the corner of Fifth and Broadway. The ground has been leased for a brickyard, and the populace objected to leave. The "eviction" yesterday was very humorous as well as affecting. But Colonel Coates made the shanties come down.
April 25

A Slice of the TIMES

-The Pacific House is being renovated from top to bottom. The front is being handsomely painted and the interior changed for the better. Mr. Hall is determined to preserve the popularity of this favorite hotel.
April 28

-The new steamer Gold Dust arrived here last night. She is the most elegant packet on the river since the steamer M. S. Mepham ran in the palmy days of steamboating. The Gold Dust ran 80 miles against wind and current yesterday. Captain Gould commands her; J. E. Tebo and Tony Burback pilots.
April 28

-Strange, but it is nevertheless true, that a very extensive willow plantation has existed within sight of this city, on the Missouri River, for several years. It is being now utilized for the first time. A few days ago a number of unemployed English people commenced to cut these willows, and now some fifteen or twenty men, women and children will go into the manufacture of basketware.
May 2

-The circus is coming. So are the pickpockets.
May 8

-Strawberries are putting in an appearance at $1 a box, and small boxes they are, too.
May 8

-Some of those citizens who have a view of the river witnessed a steamboat race yesterday morning, the first one which has been witnessed from this point for several years. The steamers General Sherman and J. Donald Cameron were the contestants. Both are very fast boats, and they plowed through the water at a great rate. The Sherman, however, was the first to reach the levee. Both steamers stayed here but a short time. They are bound for the upper river.
May 8

-The minister's boy to the West has gone - in the Black Hills you will find him; a new revolver he's girded on, and a dirk knife slung behind him.
May 8

-The prediction made by the TIMES yesterday, relative to the New Union Depot was correct. There is trouble among the railroads, and no removal will take place to the State Line until June 1st. It is more than likely that some of the roads will decline to go to the State Line; but will use their own yards and depots while the new depot is being built.
May 12

-The telephone has struck Kansas City, and the thread telegraph works like a charm. It is constructed about as follows: Take a hollow tin tube two or three inches in diameter and cover one end with muslin and glue a thread through a small hole

in the center. Fix the other end the same way, the two being attached with the thread. Thus when anything is spoken in one tube the thread transmits the sound distinctly hundreds of yards to the other tube.
May 13

-A man named Dennis Haggerty fell from the sidewalk on Union Avenue, near the Laclede Hotel, yesterday afternoon. He rolled into the gutter and then beneath the sidewalk down the bank into the pond. He would have been drowned had he not been observed when he fell. The police waded into the water and dragged him out.
May 17

-The base ball season will be formally opened to-morrow afternoon by a match game between the Athletics and Blue Stockings. The game will be played in the new base ball grounds in the Stock Exchange race course. Fine seats for spectators have been provided. Street cars run to the grounds, and everyone is invited to be present.
May 18

-There's a large margin (oleomargin) of profit in some of the butter sold in this town.
May 23

-The quoit fever is raging on the West Side.
May 23

The Brickmaker's Harvest - 1877

-A series of games of quoits for the championship of the West Side are being played this week at the quoit grounds on Tenth street, near Jefferson. The games begin each evening about 6 1/2 o'clock. Mr. Stannard, thus far, maintains the lead, though Mr. Underwood and Walter Barber are giving him a close call. Last evening young Eddy Barber entered the lists, and surprised everyone by his excellent and accurate pitching. The tally was kept last evening by one of the ladies who watched the play, which, throughout, was one of decided interest to the spectators.
May 30

Quoits is a game that, unfortunately, has not been widely remembered. Funk and Wagnalls 1913 New Standard Dictionary defines "Quoit" and "Quoits" as: "1) A circular piece of iron, with a round hole in the center, flat on one side and convex on the other, for use in playing the game of Quoits." "2) A game played by two or more persons with these disks. Two iron pins or stakes, called Hobs or Hubs, are driven into the ground at a specified distance apart; the players take position at one hub and each throws two quoits toward the opposite hub. The quoit thrown nearest the pin counts a point. If it encircles the hub it is called a ringer, and counts two or more points, as previously agreed upon."

-Another car of the Anderson Refrigerator Car Line went off last evening to Chicago with 360 dressed sheep packed within it. Here was a whole flock of sheep in one car. Make a note of this fact: this dressed meat trade is destined to become important to Kansas City and the entire West.
June 1

A Slice of the TIMES

-The great sewer being built by Mr. Halpin, in West Kansas City, is about to prove a failure. About fifty feet of the main sewer has already caved in, and the engine houses of the Fort Scott railroad are cut off from the rest of the road. The sewer is built upon quicksand and cannot be made substantial now. An open drain or sewer with sheet iron bottom is the only recourse.
June 5

-A beautiful hot house and flower garden has recently been fitted up on the corner of Oak and Twelfth streets, by R. Jarrett & Co.
June 17

-An excursion on the steamer Gold Dust is announced for next Thursday. The boat leaves at 8 a.m. Fare for the round trip to Leavenworth, 1$. Meals extra.
June 17

-The pond on the corner of Third and Grand avenue has been drained. The body of an infant was discovered in it yesterday.
June 23

-A fire broke out in the old Union Depot last night, but was unfortunately put out before it had captured the pestilential old shed.
June 23

-That Union Depot meeting did not come off. The Union Depot is like poor Sinbad the Sailor. It has got an old man of the sea upon its shoulders. Nothing but lightning, a funeral or "Father Time" will relieve Kansas City of this red tape incubus now preventing the building of the Union Depot.
June 26

-The races at Riverview Park yesterday were well attended. The track was in fine condition and some pretty good time was made during the races.
July 1

-The depot question looks a little better to-day, but as so much has been said and so little done, it isn't necessary to go into details as to what is said.
July 3

-A meeting of the indicted saloon keepers was held yesterday afternoon at Turner Hall. William Warner appeared this time when called for and made a ringing speech - such as "Windy William" only can make. The griefs of the aggrieved and the afflictions of the afflicted were painted in glowing colors, after which Mr. William Warner was retained professionally to conduct their cases in court. Wily William.
July 3

-Yesterday was the hottest day, 103 degrees in the shade.
July 7

A Slice of the TIMES

-An increased amount of sickness is reported since the hot weather set in.
July 7

-"Ise done cooked froo an' froo." remarked a perspiring darkey yesterday.
July 7

-There is no foolishness about it this time - the old Union Depot is vacated this morning.
July 8

-The trains will leave the State Line Depot this evening instead of the Union avenue shed.
July 8

-Lets all go to church to-day and thank God that the old Union Depot has been abolished.
July 8

-There will now be a general scattering of the passenger traffic to and from this city. Eastern passengers arriving and departing will prefer to use the Grand Avenue depot and the bridge depot rather than go to the State Line. Those going west and south will be obliged to use the State Line depot. The change will be a good one for hackmen and the "'bus line."
July 8

118

-The demolition of the old depot shed is being rapidly prosecuted. A large force of men were tearing it down yesterday.
July 13

-Riley, the legless bootblack at the depot, desires not to be forgotten. He says everybody else has had a mention in connection with the new depot except him.
July 13

-Alice Brown alias "Burnt-faced Mary" was arrested yesterday morning on a charge of larceny. A few days ago the house of Mr. Douglass, on the corner of Ninth and Mulberry, was robbed of some silverware, two watches and other articles of value. The officers searched the shanty of Burnt-faced Mary and found the stolen property. It is hoped that this scrape will rid the town of this chronic nuisance.
July 13

-Work on the new Lake-House Park has been commenced. The grounds will be the most attractive pleasure-grounds in this vicinity.
July 14

-Now is the time for the brickmakers harvest. Eight or nine kilns in full blast, and, as a proprietor remarked last evening, "Divil a wink o' schleep fur a man noight or day."
July 14

A Slice of the TIMES

-It is sad but true. Nearly every other married man you meet in Kansas City just now is a "grass-widower." Why is it that all the wives go east to visit friends during the summer months, leaving their disconsolate husbands, sad and forlorn, to sweat it out alone?
July 14

-The Market Master shows some inclination to be both troublesome and unobliging. It is customary for the butchers to keep meat in their ice boxes on Saturday night, for their customers (who have no ice boxes) so that they can have meat fresh for Sunday. The Market Master objects to this desecration of the Sabbath. Last Sunday he declined to admit a butcher to his own ice box, when the butch called the official a "dirty old dutch slouch." A law suit has grown out of the transaction.
July 17

-The city workhouse was never before so well handled. The farming operations are extensive and complete. The convicts prefer gardening operations to working on the streets.
July 22

-It is reported that a large amount of the funds realized from the sale of Union depot bonds arrived a day or two ago, and that work will be begun at once. The old depot is entirely removed and the ground cleared for the new building.
July 22

-Miss Helena Murray and Miss Nellie Davis will row a race from this city to Harlem and return this afternoon at 3 o'clock. The wager is a secret; but those who pretend to know say there is a young man at the bottom of it. A few personal friends of the contestants will be present.
July 22

-A raid made last night by the police upon a den of prostitution on Grand avenue resulted in the capture of five of the first sons of the first families in the city. The next time these young men are taken in by the police their names will not be withheld from publication.
August 2

-The Halpin sewer in West Kansas City, which has been interrupted by water, will now be pushed forward to a rapid completion. Dennis and John Halpin are both of them on hand and they propose making the dirt fly and that sewer assume shape. No more delay, says Dennis, "we propose finishing the job in good shape."
August 7

-As the astronomers had announced that the planet Mars would be very plainly visible yesterday morning, a large number of persons were out between midnight and 3 o'clock to enjoy a peep at the star which they say will not be plainly visible again before 1925. Most of those observed looking upwards were using the bottom of a glass.
August 16

A Slice of the TIMES

-The Kansas City elevator is giving some serious annoyance to the business men and residents on 12th street, West Kansas, and on Hickory and Wyoming streets. In cleaning the large amounts of grain passing through the elevator the dirt, dust and husks are thrown out of a chute on the south side of the building. When the wind is from the south it falls upon the almost flat roof of the elevator and is afterwards carried in clouds all over the adjoining blocks. But when the wind is from the north, there is a constant shower of dust and husks falling upon the four or five blocks of houses south of 12th street. Drug, grocery, dry goods, boot and shoe stores, and, in fact, all kinds of business houses are obliged to shut up when this shower is falling. A long petition is being prepared to the City Council to abate the nuisance.
August 16

-A prominent real estate dealer yesterday said: "I could rent one hundred small residences to-day if I had them. I was never before so badly badgered for houses." Why don't our capitalists build more residence houses?
August 23

-Michael Rowan, a well known cooper in this city, was taken sick with malarious fever last week, and being without family was taken to the Sister's Hospital on Thursday. He grew rapidly worse, being frequently delirious, and, notwithstanding the best

of care and attention given him by physicians and by the Sisters, he died Sunday night. His body was taken to Carlat's undertaking establishment and packed in ice. His funeral will take place to-day, at 2½ p.m., from Odd Fellows' Hall, under the auspices of Kansas City Lodge No. 257, of which he was a honored and highly respected member.
August 28

-There are so few of the streets of the city named that persons, strangers in the city, are frequently at a loss to find their way to any given point. Remedy it.
August 29

-On next Monday the school-bells will be heard summoning the children to school. There are nearly ten thousand school-children in the city, and it is the duty of parents to send their children to school every day, if possible. Our public schools have a reputation second to none. Let parents see to it that their children are at school first, last, and all the time. Teachers' meeting at the Central School, Saturday, 9 a.m.
August 29

-To the stranger within our gates, on a good time gaily bent, the saloons being kept open all night is a perfect God-send. And when the poison has taken due effect, the coffin shops are always open, too. Beautiful arrangement! Thus are the unities of business observed and the dependence of one branch of trade upon another strikingly illustrated.
September 1

A Slice of the TIMES

-The new Union Depot has reached the stage when carpenters are required.
September 4

-The balloon ascension from the Tivoli Garden, on Sunday afternoon was a complete success. The aerial contrivance carried up the daring tumbler on the trapeze about 5 o'clock, and came down again a short distance from the place of ascension. A large crowd witnessed the foolhardy performance.
September 4

-A large deer being chased by some boys yesterday, took refuge in the yard of a prominent west sider, who requests the owner to call at this office, pay for this advertisement, and learn where he may find his pet.
September 4

-A Press Club is the latest proposition. Why cannot the newspaper men of a small city like this meet together daily, without pistols, bowie-knives and trimmings? By all means let the Bohemians consolidate.
September 8

-Cattle killing commenced yesterday. This begins the packing season of 1877-8. The demand for cattle this year will be very large and beef packing will be pushed forward at a rapid rate. Both Russia and Turkey must have meat this winter.
September 11
Russia and Turkey were at war.

124

-By way of experiment, a lot of Joplin stone is being laid on Delaware, between Fourth and Fifth streets. It is the refuse and washings from the lead mines, and appears to be too finely pulverized to wear well. It is said that this stone will amalgamate and become as hard as solid rock. If it proves to be all that is claimed for it, the main streets of Kansas City will receive a top layer. It contains a large portion of lead and black-jack.
September 26

-Is it any wonder that this "New West" improves so rapidly? Every day there passes through this city from one to five hundred emigrants for Kansas and Colorado. On Thursday Geo. J. Clark, of the Fort Scott road, conducted 180 land buyers from Illinois to Baxter in Southern Kansas, and two days before that 700 went to Western Kansas.
September 29

-Two wicked little children amused themselves for several hours yesterday on the corner of Union avenue and Mulberry street, by exiting the cupidity of the passers by. They had a counterfeit half dollar coin, attached to a string, which they threw out as bait. The number of men who made the futile grab for the half dollar was quite surprising. The wicked children seemed to enjoy the sport.
September 29

A Slice of the TIMES

-The ordinance passed last night relative to first-class sidewalks, provides that they shall hereafter be made of brick or dressed stone. Good-by rotten wood.
October 2

-Five hundred and eighteen dollars was the amount paid into the city treasury, yesterday, by the gamblers arrested on Saturday night. No wonder the City Attorney and the Recorder went home smiling. These raids come only once a month.
October 2

-The Sisters in charge of the hospital on Penn street are endeavoring to raise means with which to furnish better bedding and other much needed accommodations for their patients. They have had a fine cow donated which is to be raffled off to raise money to assist themselves with. Of course they will be successful in their efforts.
October 2

-The raw days and chilly nights of autumn are at hand. The time of stove-pipes and stone bruises on the hands, of profanity and domestic discord on the question of where the stove shall set, of angry discussions between two hearts that beat as four or five as to where the fancy top of the heater was put - that distracting time is here. The day has arrived when the well-to-do citizen exchanges his whisky for hot Scotch, and the day laborer puts peppersauce in his beer. And, too, the day has come when, according to the New York Graphic,

"The thirsty skeeter folds his languid
  wings,
Draws in his sugur, and no longer stings;
No more artesian wells he tries to sink,
Or comes up to the bar to get a drink;
In sleep he waits another season's sup;
He's comatose; his pump is frizzen up."
October 6

-The State Line Depot was flooded last night with a crowd of returned Californians, all going East disgusted with the land of gold.
October 12

-The colored Masons of this city made a grand parade yesterday through the city. They were led by the Lexington Band (colored), and made a grand display. The occasion was the reception of Grand Master Brooks, of Kansas, who rode in an open barouche with Grand Master Andrew Hubbard, of Missouri. The Grand Lodge of the State of Kansas has been in session in Wyandotte, and last night a grand ball was given in its honor at Long's Hall in this city. It was the largest gathering of colored people ever seen in this city.
October 12

A Slice of the TIMES

-Johannes Schnappennuterrichten has obtained his divorce, and his attorney, Tom King, has prepared a petition to have his name changed to Smith.
October 20

-Two days and two nights of steady fast rain has converted Kansas City into a small edition of Venice.
October 20

-A very large cistern in the rear of the old Union Hotel caved in yesterday. It was dug in 1859, and was the largest cistern in the city. For the last six or seven years its existence has been unknown.
October 20

-The rainy weather has seriously retarded building during the past week, but it will be vigorously pushed as soon as the sun makes its appearance again. It is said there are more buildings under contract this fall than there have been since 1869, and if brick could be had, double the number would be built.
October 21

-Now for cheap meat. The proposition of Nofsinger & Harper, at the packing houses, if it is kept up during the winter, will give the people of this city a supply of good, fresh meat at half the usual price. There is no reason why beefsteaks should be sold here at higher price than in New York. "Choice cuts" can be sold here at fifty per cent advance on

wholesale cost price. Let us have cheap meat this winter. Why don't the packing houses establish a branch house up town?
October 21

-McCord, Nave and Co.'s warehouse on the corner of Santa Fe street and Union avenue fell in yesterday about noon. The joists supporting the first floor slipped out from the wall and fell into the cellar. The merchandise stored in the warehouse is being taken out and transferred to the store formerly used by Corle & Co. on Delaware street. There are other buildings in this city in immanent danger of collapsing from being over loaded.
October 24

-Yesterday morning work was resumed on the stonework of the new Union Depot. Bricks, iron and stone are being put into the building with remarkable rapidity. The walls will be ready for the roof in about one month.
October 24

-Some complaint is being made from various sources because the Mayor of the city does not pay more attention to his official duties. His office is down at the packing house, which is remote from the business center of the city. Hundreds who seek him are unable to go so far to find him. Why not have an office in the city and regular hours adopted for attendance.
October 26

-The Liverpool market is a new feature in the retail meat supply of this city. Messrs. Nofsinger, Harper & Co., of the Kansas City Packing Houses, have opened a meat market on the west side of Main street, near the "Junction." Here the best fat beef, pork and mutton is sold at retail at a slight advance on the wholesale prices at the packing houses. Kansas City is entitled to cheap meat and good meat. This city is the great meat market of the world, and there is no reason for charging a higher price for good meat here than is paid in New York, Boston or Philadelphia. A good roast of beef at 6c, or steak at 7c, is better than a roast at 10c and a steak at 15c. Hurrah for Nofsinger's Liverpool meat market. Let it be kept up.
November 4

-Scarlet fever is reported as making its ravages among the children in various portions of the city. Two deaths occurred from that cause on Sunday.
November 6

-The Mayor was authorized last night by a resolution of the City Council, to advertise for bids for lighting three hundred and thirty street lamps with kerosene, or coal oil, for the term of five years. The Council also instructed the Auditing Committee to audit no more bills of the Kansas City Gaslight and Coke Company, except for lighting the gas

lamps to date.
November 6
With the City's debt still over a million dollars, the Council looked to reducing the expenditures in lighting. They reasoned that they could either find a cheaper fuel for the lamps or force the Gas Co. to reduce its rates.

-The city went without gas last night.
November 7

-On Wednesday night the only gas lamp in the city was that of George Gaston's. It was a bright beacon which indicated enterprise.
November 9

-Snow came last night. The beautiful snow may be all nice enough as sentiment, but it is a "disgusting reality" to a reporter tramping about over the city at midnight without a friendly gas-lamp to guide him.
November 9
Due to public protest, the gas-lamps were turned on the night of November 9th. But after further disagreement with the city, the lights were turned off again the night of the 10th.

-A Kansas City man has perfected and patented a new fire-lighter or kindling. It is the best thing yet devised for lighting a fire quickly and without the danger of coal oil explosions or the trouble of chopping up kindling-wood. Mr. W. J. Huckett, an old and reliable engineer, who has been employed a year or two at the elevators, conceived the idea of utilizing corn-cobs as kindling. He invented a machine which takes out the pith or core of the cob.

Then the cob is saturated in boiling resin, and left to cool. One corn-cob will light up a coal or wood fire without kindling. A match applied to one of these cobs is sufficient. More than one hundred barrels have been sold in this city, and all pronounce them the best kindling yet invented. They are cheap, clean and handy.
November 9

-It was with an ax that Jacob Ludwig hit his wife last evening. He was arrested at his home on Third and Holmes street and brought to jail. His wife, to whom he has been married only 11 months, came to the police court to beg his release. She said she loved him too much.
November 13

-Talk of hitching up quick, the boys in No. 3 engine house are the quickest. Yesterday, while a reporter was passing the door of the house on the corner of twelfth and Walnut streets, a bell was sounded, and before he got across the front of the engine house, the hook and ladder truck dashed out. The hitching up was done in less than one minute. No. 3 challenges the West on trained horses and quick work.
November 14

-That great sensation which the Journal has been fluttering its feathers for several weeks is coming. The same sensation was raised by the Bulletin in

1870. Mr. Wm. Tobener started up the river yesterday with some friends, and will proceed to dig into the sand-bar which engulfed the steamboat Arabia and 400 barrels of whiskey. Later news will be looked for by all lovers of old whiskey.
November 14

-The laying down of new asphaltum crossings on North Main street is progressing quite rapidly. Those who have occasion to visit the new court house will now enjoy the luxury of a good crossing.
November 17

-An effort is being made to revive the almost extinct sport of rat killing. When the Levee was in its prime a rat hunt and a rat roast was one of the fashionable amusements of the young bloods of the city.
November 20

-The old buildings down on the levee are in a tottering condition and dangerous. The wood seekers have gutted the old Crowell building and are tearing out the joists. The old Globe Hotel is in a shaky condition, but is still occupied. A tragedy may be expected there before long.
November 22

-The new sewer in West Kansas City which has recently been constructed on Sante Fe street, is pronounced by competent authority to be a successful piece of engineering. It has been asserted

by many that the sewer would prove worthless for the want of sufficient fall or grade to carry off the water.
November 22

-Two pieces of Mexican silver coin were washed out in a deep gully north of the new court house during the late rains. One of the coins bears the date of 1826. This is a portion of some hidden treasure, long sought for but never found, except by the rain. There has been about forty picked up in the ravine during the last five years.
November 22

-There have been several new propositions made to light the city. Gas will be cheaper hereafter.
November 23

-All the gas and gasoline lamps were lighted on the public square last night. And still the moon was brightly shining.
November 23
To help decide whether to use gas or gasoline (coal oil) to light the city, both types were used in the square for comparison.

-Those who got drunk on Thanksgiving day or night were exempt from arrest by the police.
December 1

-The gas question is settled.
December 4

-Twenty new gas lamps are to be removed to new locations.
December 4

-Bluff street and East Ninth street are to be illuminated with new gas lamps.
December 4
The City Council decided to use a combination of gas and gasoline lamps. The majority of the gas lamps would remain, while new lamps would be of the cheaper gasoline burning variety.

-The hog season was formally opened yesterday by the slaughter of 1,300 head by Slavens, Mansur & Co. This house has ceased to kill beef and will turn its attention to hogs for the balance of the season.
December 4

-The fixing of the location of the 110 gasoline lamps is a task that will tax the judgement of the gas committee.
December 7

-Thirty-eight thousand tons of ice is required for the local trade of Kansas City next year.
December 9

-A pop corn ball manufactory is the latest thing out in Kansas City. N. W. Becroff is the proprietor, and his work is excellent.
December 9

-Speaking of new improvements, the enterprising proprietor of the Coates House, Col. Kersey Coates, is about to enlarge his palatial hotel by the erection of a large wing upon the southern side, thus completing the original design of the architect.
December 18

-They are importing brick from all the surrounding country. Next year Kansas City will try and make brick enough to do her citizens.
December 19

The Coates House Hotel after the expansion.

A Test of Temperance
1878

The Murphy Temperance Movement in Kansas City gained many followers in 1878. Their revival-styled meetings and eloquent speakers helped many give up alcohol and don the Blue Ribbon. But Kansas City was a hard town to temper, and the temptation of cheap whiskey or a "schooner" of beer (and the free lunch that came with it) was too much for many in the community. The Movement did have other successes, however. The city's first drinking fountains, located primarily in the saloon districts, were due, in large part, to the efforts of the Temperance people. And by 1885, their support was strong enough to push legislation through in Kansas, making it a dry state.

In the South, a massive outbreak of Yellow Fever claimed some 14,000 lives before it was abated by the cold of winter. Kansas City participated in world-wide relief efforts and sent thousands of dollars for food and medicine. In all, some $400,000 in cash, as well as clothing, supplies and medical assistance were donated to the hardest hit areas of Louisiana, Alabama, Mississippi and Tennessee. It was a tragedy that Kansas City would learn from.

A Test of Temperance - 1878

-An attempt was made on Wednesday night to burn the residence of Mr. Nathan Scarritt, about a mile east of the city. There was a party in the house, and while all were enjoying themselves below some rascal went up stairs and built a fire upon the bed in one room and another fire between the plaster and the weatherboarding in another room. With the aid of the young men at the party the building was saved, with damage of a few hundred dollars. A negro vagrant, who was shot at while the house was burning, is said to have been the originator of the fire.
January 4

-An alarm was given about half past six last night, caused by a man climbing over the fence of the jail yard in the rear of the new court house. The police rallied promptly, supposing it to be an emeute from the county jail. Investigation reported it as the jailer climbing the fence in pursuit of a truant hog.
January 10

-Seven thousand hogs in one day is the latest report from the livestock circles.
January 11

-The Rev. Armstrong will preach a temperance sermon in Kansas City, Ks. at the Union Church, this morning, at 11 o'clock.
January 13

A Slice of the TIMES

-When the front wall of the old Globe Hotel, on the levee, fell yesterday two men narrowly escaped being buried in the ruins.
January 17

-There was a strike yesterday among the men at work tearing down the old buildings on the levee. They refused to work for less than $1.50 per day. In two hours there were at least fifty men anxious to work for $1.25.
January 17

-Plastering has been commenced in the new Union Depot, and the steam apparatus is in full blast. Mr. McGonigle, the contractor, is pushing on the work at a rapid rate.
January 17

-The gambling houses were crowded last night - the pay cars having just been about.
January 20

-The first section of "first class sidewalk," according to the new law, was laid yesterday on Delaware street, between Third and Fourth. It is of brick, with stone crossing. It is first class.
January 20

-Mr. Shelton delivered a temperance address at St. John's Chapel, West Kansas City, Saturday evening, forty signing the pledge.
January 22

140

A Test of Temperance - 1878

-A telephone line is being erected from the First National to the Stock Yard Bank. The business between the two banks is of such a character that the telegraph is often too slow.
January 22

-Two or three large brick making firms will be established here in the spring. Brick, however, will not be obtainable here before May next at less than $3 per 1,000.
January 22

-Boulevard lamps of the latest style are being placed on Main street. They are very handsome and have a metropolitan appearance. It is the intention of the Gas company to replace the old lamps all over the city with this crystal globe.
January 22

-The temperance movement was inaugurated at Wyandotte Grove Church Sunday evening by Mr. Shelton. An enthusiastic audience greeted him, and every one present except four signed the Murphy pledge and donned the blue ribbon.
January 22

-It may appear funny, remarkably so to some of our fellow citizens who do not agree with the people who are engaged in the present temperance reform, to tie blue ribbons on their dogs, and no doubt it is; yet when a man parades the streets intoxicated to a degree bordering on the beastly, followed by a

forlorn dog which he has decorated with a blue ribbon, it is enough to arouse the sympathy of anybody for the dog. It looks as if the dumb brute was in terrible bad company. If a person does not agree with the reformers it is better that he keep quiet, and especially is it meet that he does nothing that will lead the public to belive him narrow-minded and foolish. Every man has a right to drink if he so desires, but a man should not, nor yet will a real man, make himself appear foolish or ridiculous.
January 22

-J. Kiser has completed the largest piece of marble perhaps, in the West, for toilet purposes. It is three feet wide, and eighteen feet long, containing eight basins for washing purposes, made out of pure imported Italian marble, and will grace the main entrance of the new Union Depot.
January 26

-Contracts were let yesterday to Jas. Dowling & Brother for the stonework of a new five story building on the corner of Sixth and Deleware streets. The building is to be one hundred and ten feet deep and forty feet wide, five stories high and will have a dressed stone front. The building is the enterprise of T. M. James & Sons. It will be one of the largest and handsomest buildings in Kansas City. Nothing like enterprise to build up a city.
January 27

A Test of Temperance - 1878

-This evening, at Liberty Street M. E. Church, addresses will be made by Rev. J. P. Dew and others. Several reformed drinkers will relate their experiences, including one gentleman who has been a drinking man for forty years and signed the pledge a few evenings ago at Franks Hall. The choir has prepared some new temperance songs for the occasion, and good music may be expected.
January 27

-Ice men seem to have abandoned all hope of getting ice here this season. Yesterday afternoon Sales, Orbison and others left for Council Bluffs with a view to getting a crop of ice at that point and shipping it here.
January 30

-On careful estimate, it is found that every home in "Hell's Half-Acre" has three dogs.
January 30

-It was thought that when the Black Jack was placed upon Deleware street that that would be the "boss" street of the city; that mud would not accumulate thereon. This theory, has proven a falasy since the duration of the soft weather, as there seems to be as much mud there as on any other macadamized street in the city.
February 3

-The sum of $8,500.38 was what it cost Kansas City to run the municipal machine last year.
February 5

A Slice of the TIMES

-Stonework on the new buildings in various portions of the city was recommenced yesterday. The roads have been so bad that hauling has been almost impassible for about two weeks.
February 5

-Catherine street died last night. This morning it will be known officially as Madison Avenue.
February 5

-Building throughout the city is progressing nicely, but has for some days past been greatly interfered with by the wet weather. It is anticipated that when spring fairly opens, there will be greater activity among our builders than has been known for years. The outlook hence, is extremely cheering to the mechanics and laboring classes.
February 14

-The iron for the new veranda of the Union Depot is now being put up at the west end.
February 16

-The people residing in the neighborhood of the bone factory on the east bottom complain loudly of the very bad odor which emanates from that institution. It is unfortunate indeed that the fertilizing institution cannot be run without being a nuisance to those who reside in its vicinity. It cannot do so, it seems, and just so long as there may arise from it a foul and unhealthy odor, just so long will those tormented with such a nuisance be

complaining. Better do something to kill the scent.
February 16

-Work has been commenced for the demolition of the old warehouse on the levee known as the Crowell building.
February 23

-The Rev. Father Dalton spoke again on intemperance in the Presbyterian church, West Kansas, and his remarks were not only well received but much applauded, especially when he advocated the union of all, irrespective of creeds or denominations, in the grand work of humanity. He was followed by Mr. Thompson, who said he thought it nothing but fair something be said on the other side, and made many good and laughable illustrations, which brought down the house, and if he did not convince the audience of his theory it was no fault of his.
February 23

-The dome of the new Union Depot was being put up yesterday.
February 27

-Dog and chicken fights are the chief amusements on West 9th and Santa Fe streets, West Kansas. A lively dog fight was yesterday witnessed in that locality, by over forty people and betting going on freely.
February 28

A Slice of the TIMES

-During the past year the receipts of grain in St. Louis were 3,795,166 bushels less than for 1876; while Kansas City gained 783,518 bushels in the same period. Anybody can make his own comment on the above facts.
March 1

-The topic of the town yesterday was of Green, and his swift approaching doom. It will prove again the chief topic of conversation to-day from morning till night.
March 1

-Parents who regard the welfare of their children should keep their boys away from the Court House this morning. There is not only danger of the youngsters being injured, but the scene that will be presented is not such an one as a child should witness.
March 1

At about 10:15 AM, March 1, Kansas City held its first judicial execution. It was only the second in the history of Jackson County, the last being in 1839. The convicted man, Richard Green (alias McFerran), was hanged for the murder of Deputy Marshal Henry M. Hughes. The execution took place behind the Court House. Marshal Liggett issued 150 tickets to the press, physicians and specially invited guests. Even with this controlled attendance, nearly the entire town turned out to watch from windows and rooftops.

-Railway companies are now getting short of cars, such is the amount of travel coming West.
March 6

A Test of Temperance - 1878

-The Kansas City Temperance Union open their new hall in West Kansas City, to-night. Several prominent temperance speakers are expected to attend the meeting. Rev. Father Dalton will deliver the opening address.
March 7

-Packing houses have almost stopped killing, the warm weather making it risky work to slaughter.
March 8

-It is announced that Plankinton & Armours will shortly build another addition to their already immense establishment, on the northeast corner of their packing-house; and that in all likelihood they will put up corn beef, hams, etc., in tins, as done by the preserved meat firms of Chicago, Ill.
March 9

-Work has been commenced in nearly all the brick-yards. With a continuation of good weather, there will soon be an abundance of building-material on hand.
March 10

-Jack Mahoney, who lives on Liberty street, West Kansas, had a very sick cow a few nights since, and one of his friends advised him to get a pint of whisky and pour it down the cow's throat. Now, Jack had been suffering with a severe cold, so he went and got a quart of good whisky. He gave the

cow half, and - well, Jack and the cow both recovered.
March 10

-Register to-day, or lose your vote in the city election.
March 13

-The new fashion for ladies dresses is meeting with much favor. Short skirts for street wear will be all the rage.
March 13

-For several weeks past Superintendent Sheppard, of the Workhouse, has kept his manacled convicts from the streets where a chain-gang was offensive to the public taste. The convicts have been kept at work breaking stone, which yields to the city about one dollar per day each man. This will repair the streets and yield to the city some remuneration for the expense of feeding its convicts.
March 14

-The chairs, seats, etc., for the new Union Depot came to hand yesterday.
March 16

-The ghost show still flourishes! It now occupies the building formerly used by E. Steine, as a coffin repository. A good place for ghosts.
March 16

A Test of Temperance - 1878

-Mr. Clay Crenshaw has just completed arrangements for the erection of the largest horse and mule stables in the West. The building will be 100x110 feet, and will be located at the corner of Washington and Fifth streets, and will be opened out as the Planters Horse and Mule Market.
March 21

-Little Charlie Moran, aged about six years, living in the hollow back of the Coates Opera House, met with an accident yesterday afternoon while out at play which is likely to result in his death. He was attacked by a cow which run him down and gored him in the groin, tearing the flesh in a most fearful manner. No child is safe upon the streets where so many cows and horses are allowed to run at large.
March 22

-They will commence, to-day, putting up the local ticket case in the ticket office at the Union depot.
March 26

-The new depot will be dedicated one week from yesterday - April 6th.
March 31

-Several lively knock-downs occurred, yesterday, during the polling at the Sixth Ward, which resulted in some arrests being made. No person was seriously hurt.
April 3

A Slice of the TIMES

-The city election excitement calmed down quite suddenly. To look about the streets yesterday no one would for a moment suppose that there had been an election on the day preceeding. Everybody seemed to be satisfied with the result.
April 4

-The skeletons of old pioneers and early settlers buried in the old city graveyard on Independence avenue still offend the eyes of the sensitive. The work of removing the dead was commenced some years ago, but abandoned, and the bones of fifteen or twenty persons left in a box until a citizen put it under ground. It is not right to see the skulls and bones of human beings exposed to sight on the principal streets of a city.
April 4

-The finishing touches were being put to the new Union Depot yesterday.
April 7

-The old State Line Depot was nearly deserted yesterday. Carpenters and others are busy pulling down and tearing away matters and removing them to new quarters. At midnight last night all was deserted and the old State Line Depot was a thing of the past.
April 7

-The new depot was crowded yesterday with spectators and travelers.
April 9

150

A Test of Temperance - 1878

-The remarks in yesterday's TIMES in regard to the small-pox, has had its weight with the city officials. It was noticed, yesterday, that all the houses infected with the disease, in West Kansas, had a notice of "small-pox" pasted on the door.
April 11

-The colored people gave a festival at Turner Hall last night for the benefit of the colored Young Men's Literary Club of this city.
April 12

-Why do people go so far west to buy land when fine, improved farms can be bought within twenty miles of Kansas City for $16 per acre.
April 12

-Mayor Shelley will fit up, furnish and occupy an office in the old Court House during his term of office. He proposes to be Mayor in fact as well as in name.
April 17

-An immense hog took possession of the sidewalk on Santa Fe street near St. Louis avenue, and remained there all day to the annoyance of pedestrians.
April 19

-The Union ticket-office, at the depot, has tickets on hand valued at nearly $5,000,000. Their average sales are from $1,800 to $4,000 per day.
April 20

A Slice of the TIMES

-In consequence of the prevalence of small-pox in certain localities in West Kansas, the public schools have been closed during the last week or two, but commenced their usual exercises on Monday.
April 24

-A young man was at the depot yesterday with anklets on, in charge of the Deputy Sheriff from Fort Scott, who was taking him to Jefferson City, at which place he is to serve two years' imprisonment for stealing $50.
April 24

-Make a note of it. There are now fourteen beer bottling establishments in the city, and still the people complain that they do not get enough beer.
May 4

-Preparations are being made for fencing, grading and ornamenting the old cemetery lot on Independence avenue. The workhouse gang will be put to work on it tomorrow. Trees will be planted, fences built, and the place made more sightly and respectable.
May 5

-The scaffolding at the depot was all taken down yesterday. Parties can take their promenade without the cry of "heads" reaching them in all directions.
May 5

A Test of Temperance - 1878

-The committee on the ball to-morrow (Friday) night, in Freeman's Hall, are all young men of good standing, which will inure an excellent time. The music, "The West End Band," is composed of some of the best musical talent in the city.
May 9

-Simmy Kelly and Bobby Potee had a little fun all to themselves on Fourth street the other night. It was a wager: Kelly was to pack Potee on his back from Main street to the Theater Comique. Kelly did all he contracted to do, followed by a large and enthusiastic crowd. He offered to carry his passenger into the crowded theater, but Potee objected.
May 9
When the legislature passed an anti-gambling law in 1881, Bob Potee put on his best clothes and drowned himself in the Missouri river. He wanted nothing to do with a Kansas City without gambling. But his conclusion was hasty; gambling continued in Kansas City for many years.

-The ice trade is about to assume a new and interesting phase. A cut in the contract rates is assured, which will bring that luxury down to 75 cents per hundred pounds.
May 10

-The work on the old cemetery on Independence avenue is progressing steadily each day.
May 17

A Slice of the TIMES

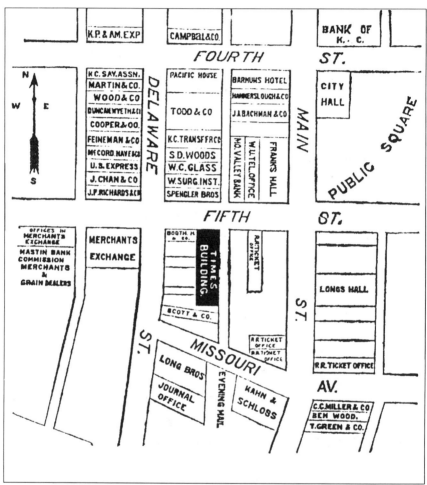

The TIMES ran this map on May 12, 1878, to show the location of their new
building in "the business center of Kansas City."

A Test of Temperance - 1878

-To-night the Temperance Union give another of those delightful parties at their hall. The West End band will furnish the music, and those who attend are insured a "jolly good time."
May 17

-There was a ludicrous fight on the Public Square yesterday between a hog and a mule. The dispute was about some corn, which had been fed to the mule by a farmer, and which the hog insisted upon sharing. The mule - which was a very large one - attempted to settle the despute by seizing the hog with its capacious jaws, and lifting it up and throwing it half across the street. The hog returned to the charge, but was soon settled by several heavy kicks.
May 17

-Wm. Weston, the City Treasurer, has established a telephone wire between his office at Harburg's store, on the corner of Main street and Missouri avenue, and his lime kiln in the east edge of the city. This will be a great convenience for those employed in the business as well as for builders ordering lime.
May 18

-An effort is being made by outside interested parties to have Officer Davis removed from the police force. He is one of the best now on the force and his removal would be a great loss. His color has not prevented him becoming one of the best police officers in the city.
May 18
Davis is thought to be the first black police officer in the City.

A Slice of the TIMES

-The damage done to the new foundation of T. M. James & Sons, on Delaware and Sixth streets, by the late rains, will not be less than $500. The Gas Company removed its lamp-post just before another land slide occurred. The Corrigan Street railway line is somewhat damaged. A new turntable and switch will be required.
May 19

-Valentine Love, the enterprising proprietor of the Theatre Comique, is the proud owner of the scalp of the notorious Cheyenne chief "Grey Wolf," who distinguished himself and became infamous by the massacre of the German family seven years ago. The scalp is a fine one, and is well tanned.
May 19

-City Engineer Trowbridge reports the discovery of a large number of skeletons where his men are at work grading the old pioneer cemetery. As each body is discovered the bones are carefully gathered together and placed in a new pine coffin, and reinterred upon the site of the original grave. The removal is caused by grading down the surface of the old graveyard. As there are no grave-stones or records, the bodies are numbered as they are found, and a stake with the number on it placed at the head.
May 22

-The new Asphaltum crossings in West Kansas are spreading themselves all over the street. A few more hot days and they can be scooped out of the gutters.
May 24

A Test of Temperance - 1878

-Thirty-one skeletons, evidently full-grown males, were discovered yesterday by the men at work excavating on Independence avenue. They were all in one grave. A large box was provided by the City Engineer and the remains reinterred.
May 30

-It was stated yesterday afternoon that the coopers had received another cut. This will bring down the rate of wages to about a dollar a day.
June 5

-An Italian with a hand-organ was grinding out some music to the denizens of the bottoms yesterday. The nickels not coming in very fast, he soon left in disgust.
June 5

-Where are the summer steamboat excursions this year? Where's the Golddust, and who will start the first river ride this season?
June 6

-Our citizens should turn out to-day and this evening to give the Kansas scientists a fitting reception. Go with them to the mounds this morning, at 8 o'clock, and take your lunch baskets with you. The party will gather at the St. James. A drive into the country will be delightful and a peep into the mounds will be unique.
June 7

A Slice of the TIMES

-Placards, warning travelers of thieves and confidence men, have been placed in the Union depot.
June 12

-There is no happier man in the city just now than ex-Alderman Edward Kelly, the well known proprietor of the Mechanics' Hotel. He returned from Ireland about nine months ago with a handsome little wife, and now he is the father of a fine, bouncing girl. Congratulations are in order.
June 13

-Special tax bills amounting to about $25,000 are being prepared to collect the amount necessary to pay for the large sewer built last winter in West Kansas City.
June 14

-The pest house on the island below the city is reported to be in great danger from the high water. There are seven or eight patients there who ought to be attended to.
June 14

-The City Engineer is complying with the instructions given by the City Council to remove obstructions from sidewalks. His men were engaged yesterday and Wednesday in pulling down stairways and bill boards on Fifth street.
June 14

-The scientists intend to make another visit to the Clay county mounds in a few days under the lead and guidance of Dr. Chaifant, who has some hidden treasures to reveal.
June 15

-The men engaged in excavating the old graveyard on Independence avenue yesterday discovered the remains of a woman buried thirty-six years ago. Her hair was about fifteen inches long and flax colored.
June 15

-There was a remarkable stretch of authority developed on Thursday night upon the part of a police officer on Main street. A party of musicians and comedians stopped in Rielly's on their way home from the theater. There they indulged in a little music and one or two songs, when an officer stepped into the saloon and endeavored to arrest the party. The barkeeper protested, and bade the too officious guardian of the peace to step outside and watch his beat, and wait until he was invited to make arrests. The police have just the same right to enter private houses and put a stop to dances and home concerts, as to enter a saloon to stop a social concert among musicians which annoyed no one but the patrolling officer.
June 20

A Slice of the TIMES

-The attention of the City Physician is called to a house standing next to Moriarty's grocery store, Ninth street, West Kansas, over the door of which has been put a sign, "Small-pox here." This house is small, and has for its occupants a colored family who are down with the terrible disease. It is situated almost right on the sidewalk, and every person who passes that way must almost rub their clothes against the building. The parties who are down with the sickness should be instantly removed to the pest house or some isolated dwelling, and not allowed to spread that contagious malady over the entire neighborhood.
June 21

-The City Recorder very properly dismissed the charges made against the young men of the Theatre Comique. They were arrested for singing and playing music in Rielley's saloon, with the full consent of the proprietor. Prof. Keickhoffer, the leader of the orchestra, appeared as counsel in the case, and made a first class argument.
June 22

-An amusing game of base ball will be played this afternoon on the Eighteenth street grounds. The game is between the lean and fat members of the Board of Trade Building. Fat men's nine are as follows: R. E. Talpey, Web Withers, J. C. Meyers, Bucklin, J. W. Kyle, C. E. Kearney, B. Hall, Joe Underwood and C. S. Lee. The leans will be

160

represented by W. B. Barber, J. W. Titus, J. E. Seaver, Schroeder, Threlkeld, Graff, Nip Allen, J. C. Acheson and E. W. Smith. Game called at 3:30 p.m.
June 22

-J. T. Sargent will exhibit Edison's wonderful phonograph, or talking machine, to-day and to-morrow, at the Live Stock Exchange, being on exhibition the entire day. It was visited by large numbers in Wyandotte, and pronounced by all the wonder of the age.
June 26

-Six thousand dollars worth of ones and twos of the city greenbacks are to be redeemed with United States greenbacks next month.
June 29

-D. S. Harriman left his rat terrier in room No. 2, Merchants' Exchange, last Monday night. During the thirty minutes it was in the room the dog killed fifteen large rats. Whose dog can beat that?
July 3

-Among the few accidents attributable to the festivities of the Fourth was one which befell the little daughter of Mrs. Mason, of Lawrence, now on a visit to the family of Capt. Joseph Gibbs. Mrs. Mason and daughter were out on the Exposition Grounds witnessing the fireworks, when a stick fell

from an exploded rocket and broke the little girl's arm. Dr. G. E. Heydon was called upon and administered relief to the little sufferer.
July 6

-By all means, let us have a few drinking fountains located upon the principal streets.
July 7

-Yesterday, while Howe's Circus was passing through Main street, a thief entered Mr. Diveley's store, on the corner of Third and Main, and tapped the money drawer. Money and drafts to the amount of over $300 was taken by the agile thief. Merchants should be more careful when the circus is in town, as a large number of them follow such combinations.
July 7

-Mulberry street, near St. Louis avenue, West Kansas, looks like a vast brick yard.
July 12

-There are some twenty brick business buildings going up in West Kansas at the present time.
July 12

-More brick, is the continued call in West Kansas.
July 12

A Test of Temperance - 1878

-Major Blossom intends putting in coal oil lamps at the depot for the purpose of lighting up the eating stand at night.
July 12

-"Maple Grove Station" is the name of a new village just started between this city and Independence on the Narrow Gauge Railroad.
July 12

-The workhouse gang ceased its work on the old grave yard, and will now confine its operations to quarrying rock for the repairs on the main sewer on the public square.
July 16

-A man floated down the river past the city yesterday upon two logs braced together by a board, upon which he was seated. He was using a paddle to increase his speed and said he was bound for New Orleans.
July 19

-The platform at the Union Depot was kept dampened during yesterday by Depot Master Friedenburg, and added much to the comfort of passengers.
July 20

-During the hot spell Cosbey sold about a barrel of lemonade daily at the depot.
July 23

A Slice of the TIMES

-A number of tramps, to the annoyance of many, are found at all times lying under the bluff opposite the Union Depot; they should be made to vacate.
July 23

-This morning at 4 o'clock Mayor Shelley will lead the City Council, with the City Engineer and newspaper reporters, down through the main sewers of the city. Whew! what a pleasure excursion to take just before breakfast.
July 24

-The friends of Mr. Ed Kelley, of the Mechanics' Hotel, will regret to hear of the death of his only child and the serious illness of his wife. The child died yesterday at one o'clock. The funeral will take place to-day.
July 26

-There has been a fine brick pavement laid along the east side of Broadway, from the Coates House to Seventh street, and a fill is now being made on the west side, for the purpose of treating it to a like pavement.
July 28

-What is the matter with the hog law? Still this great nuisance to the general public is unabated, and the hogs still root, grunt and wallow in the hundreds of cess pools of pestilence with which our city abounds, making them as well as the hogs doubly offensive.
July 28

A Test of Temperance - 1878

-The eclipse yesterday excited considerable curiosity and was witnessed by nearly every one of the fifty thousand people in Kansas City.
July 30

-Smoked glass was all the rage yesterday.
July 30

-To-morrow is emancipation day. The colored people will have a grand parade and picnic, and a large number of people are expected from abroad. Excursions from Liberty, Independence, Leavenworth, Lawrence, and Wyandotte will visit the city. Col. John T. Crisp and R. T. Van Horn have been invited to deliver orations.
July 31

-50,126. That is the statement of the present population of Kansas City, as made by Messrs. Ballenger & Hoye, publishers of the Kansas City Directory. Their canvass of the city ended on the 1st of last month, and their figures of the actual population of the town are entirely accurate. Let it be recorded that Kansas City has now a population of over 50,000.
August 4

-What had you in the Mastin Bank? was the question in West Kansas yesterday.
August 4
After a steady four day "run" by the major depositors, uncertain of the bank's stability, the Mastin Bank found itself

A Slice of the TIMES

with insufficient funds to open for business on the 3rd. The Mastin Bank was one of the oldest banks in Kansas City and held deposits from the City, County and State. Kersey Coates was appointed assignee of the bank.

-Those who exulted the loudest over the closing of the Mastin Bank are now vociferous in their demand for silence concerning the causes leading to the calamity.
August 8

-The continued hot weather is almost unbearable.
August 8

-The infant child of W. O'Connell died yesterday in West Kansas.
August 8

-The Fort Scott checks have all of them stamped on the front: "Payable at Mastin Bank, or payable at First National Bank, Fort Scott." Some of the men were tempted, yesterday, when they got their pay, to see what could be done with a check on a busted bank, but on going to the Union depot ticket office they got them cashed, and all were happy.
August 9

-Don't fret and stew about the hot weather, as we are well assured by the astronomers that in seven thousand years the earth will be as cold as a setter pup's nose.
August 10

166

A Test of Temperance - 1878

-Talk about beer-drinking, the firm of Stiefel & Ney last month sold twenty-five car loads of Anhauser's beer in this city. This is only one of five or six beer agencies in this city.
August 10

-We are indebted to Mr. A. C. Stein, Nos. 3 and 5 Missouri avenue, for the first fresh oysters of the season. They were nice "Phat" fellows. Stein is always first in all the good things calculated to tickle the palates of mortals.
August 17

-A malicious report was started yesterday that a run was taking place on the Bank of Kansas City. It was false in every particular.
August 20

-The city has been overrun with cow boys during the past few days.
August 20

-Considerable excitement was created on the Public Square yesterday afternoon by some cow boys, who were selling ponies. A large crowd gathered, and the fun was enjoyed by everyone.
August 21

-Crazy Alice was released from the county jail yesterday, and is now skipping around the railroad yards in West Kansas once more.
August 22

A Slice of the TIMES

-The well known young attorney who frequently visits a three story brick building on Main street, should see to it that the blinds are closed next time.
August 22

-Col. Kersey Coates promises to make a statement to the public of the condition of the Mastin Bank just as soon as possible, but thinks it will be nearly a month before he will be enabled to so do.
August 25

-A method of show window decoration, which seems to be growing in favor, is that of inserting photographs of popular actresses, and it is no longer confined to the stationary trade, as heretofore.
September 5

-If parties who come down to the Union Depot with their rigs, could be made to tie their animals to some hitching post, and not leave them standing, the run-aways would be of less frequent occurrence.
September 12

-An unfortunate woman arrived last evening at the depot, having with her ten children. She wished to get a place to lodge, and the moment she placed her foot inside the depot she was besieged by a number of hotel runners, who fairly bewildered the woman and jostled her about till she sought refuge at the nearest hotel. Such proceedings should be put a stop to.
September 13

A Test of Temperance - 1878

-The law which prevents the removal of the body, in the case of death from unknown cause, before the arrival of the coroner, is doubtless founded in good reason, but it has defects, and one of them was apparent last night, when for half an hour the idle crowd was permitted to gratify its unworthy curiosity in the inspection of Cooper's body lying dead upon the sidewalk.
September 21

-The Fanny Lewis arrived yesterday morning from below, and after delivering her freight at the levee, started through the draw with a barge loaded with ties, which she had in tow. The wind was very high and directly down the river, and the boat was nearly seventy-five minutes in getting through, detaining train No. 10 of the North Missouri for over an hour. When a short distance above the bridge the wind drove the barge upon the shore and badly damaged its hull.
September 26

-Malarial fever is slightly prevalent in the city. Care should be taken to avoid undue exposure to sudden changes of temperature.
September 27

-The melancholy days have come,
    The saddest of the year,
When watermelons and ice cream
    Begin to disappear;

A Slice of the TIMES

Soda and lemonade have flown,
And pop has passed away;
In vain for iced tea one may call
Through all the autumn day.
September 27

-The "heated term" has passed; the "times that fried men's soles" are gone by - for a few months any how.
September 28

-A dead cow now ornaments part of the ground near the M. P. round house, West Kansas. As every one has taken a good look at the dead bovine, it might now be removed.
September 28

-"Has Kansas City a crack base ball nine?" Nein.
September 28

-A milkman's trust in the integrity of wayfaring humanity seems always great when he leaves the unguarded lacteal behind to seek the kitchen door and the housemaid, and that of a Sixth street vender was shamefully abused yesterday morning by a passing tramp, who paused and drank from the cream cap about a half a gallon of that precious fluid in the absence of the owner.
October 4

A Test of Temperance - 1878

-Kansas City firemen ought to be getting fat. At any rate they have very little exercise. Was ever a town as large as this so free for years from the visit of "the fiend?" Nay, verily.
October 4

-Considerable excitement was occasioned in a West Kansas saloon by a mounted stranger, who rode up to the door, got off his horse, entered and procured a drink and then throwing back his coat and showing a belt full of pistols announced that he was Cole Younger, that there was $10,000 reward for his apprehension, and dared any one to attempt his arrest. No one dared and the stranger rode away toward the Kaw before the astonished bar keeper had collected his drink fee.
October 5

-The postoffice ought to wear a sign to indicate its whereabouts. Strangers who are looking for it pass it every day without the remotest suspicion that it is where it is, and old residents are bored a dozen times to the block, whenever on the street, by inquiries as to its location. Hang your banner on the outer wall.
October 6

-A meeting of the persons interested in the project of raising the whisky lost in the Missouri river above Wyandotte, in '57, was yesterday held at Barnum's Hotel. The exact spot is said to have been

found, and the barrels discovered beneath about twenty feet of sand, the river channel having shifted since the boat sank. There are said to be 580 barrels, of 40 gallons each. A competent engineer will soon make an examination of the spot and estimate the cost of sinking a caisson in the quicksand.
October 12

-Mayor Shelley and City Engineer Trowbridge are completing arrangements for fencing and grassing the Cemetery Park on Independence avenue, and it is hoped that the people in the First ward especially, will see to it that trees are planted, and the park otherwise beautified.
October 15
This was to be the city's first public park. It cost nothing for the land, and very little for beautification.

-Arrangements have been made by Mayor Shelley for the immediate building of a fence about the Cemetery Park on Independence avenue, and for the beautifying of the same in various ways. Trees are to be planted, grass is to be sown and in a year or two it will become a popular summer resort. Yesterday Mr. Shelley received a letter from Mr. Val. Love of the Theatre Comique, enclosing an order for $25.00 to be used in beautifying the Park as was deemed best by Mr. Sheeley.
October 19

A Test of Temperance - 1878

-The sheriff of Cass county was in the city yesterday. The murderer, Issacs, is to be hanged by him on Friday next, and he wished to inspect the construction of the gallows at the jail here.
October 22

-On Sunday night burglars entered the houses of D. P. Etue and M. H. Stevens, securing at the latter place a watch and revolver, with which they escaped undetected. It is true that Kansas City has a reputation to sustain, but house-breaking is becoming an altogether too frequent occurrence in this city, even if it is the western metropolis.
October 22

-The short-skirted walking dress for street wear has come into very general use by the Kansas City ladies wearing less than a No. 6 boot.
October 25

-"Vote early and often" should to-day be the watchword of every noble and true-hearted American citizen.
November 5

-The opening of the great organ recently put in St. Luke's Church will be made on Thursday evening next, and a grand organ concert will then take place. Bach Bros. of Leavenworth, Prof. Fiske and Prof. Eoff, will take part.
November 5

A Slice of the TIMES

-And now that the election is over, let that sign be put on the postoffice building.
November 7

-Did you put a pecuniary estimate on your judgment regarding the result of the election? And have you bet-tered yourself thereby?
November 7

-The stereopticon man draws big crowds to his nightly exhibition at the corner of Fifth and Main streets. It is a novel method of advertising, and seems to be quite a success in its way.
November 7
The "stereopticon" was an early version of a slide projector, and was considered an improved "magic lantern."

-The special police of West Kansas are greatly annoyed by the number of young children sent by their parents to gather coal in the various railway yards. It is not only highly dangerous for the children to be digging about between the cars, but it is teaching them the first steps to pilfering.
November 13

-The sidewalk on the north side of Fifth street, between Main and Delaware, is being relaid with brick.
November 14

174

A Test of Temperance - 1878

-The funeral of an infant daughter of Major and Mrs. L. K. Thacher took place yesterday afternoon from the house on Eleventh street, the services being attended by a large number of sympathizing friends.
November 14

-A new and startling method adopted by ye dry goods man of displaying fancy hosiery in their show-windows, consists in stuffing the same with cotton and presenting them to view, with much the appearance of reality. The windows appear to have many admirers.
November 16

-There is scarcely a residence street in the city upon which a number of handsome new brick houses are not in course of erection or but recently completed.
November 21

-The free-lunch men are striving as to which shall give the biggest spread for a nickel. For this price you can now purchase a schooner of beer and have a square meal and trimmings thrown in.
November 21

-The city engineer wishes to inform those persons who have been hauling wagon loads of broken crockery, dismantled oyster cans, the wreck of what was once glassware, and other articles of that nature, to the new park and there dumping them,

that no such compost is needed to adorn that spot and further contributions of that nature are declined with thanks.
November 22

-A singular bet was made yesterday by two well-known gentlemen, as to what place made the best coffee. Accompanied by the referee they visited the various places, and finally wound up at Major Blossom's, at the depot, which was pronounced the best, and the loser paid his bet, $10, like a little man.
November 27

-Places of business throughout the city will be very generally closed this afternoon. Persons wishing to procure materials for their Thanksgiving dinner at the market house, should remember that it closes after 9 a.m.
November 28

-It takes nearly 300 bushels of coal per week to heat up the Union depot building.
December 1

-The question whether or not the fire department shall be permitted to fill cisterns for citizens is an interesting one for housekeepers.
December 4

A Test of Temperance - 1878

-Some boys, with bean-shooters, are doing considerable damage to windows in various parts of the city, by shooting bullets through them. The residence of Mr. Sedgewick was victimized in this way by a number of panes of glass being broken in front of his house.
December 5

-It is said that the basement of the new Bank of Kansas City building will be used for a billiard hall.
December 7

-The funeral procession for the late Dennis Halpin, yesterday morning, was one of the largest seen in this city for a long time past, being nearly three quarters of a mile in length.
December 13

-Sunday was a delightful day for sleigh riding and a great day for the sleigh riders. As on the Sunday before, the streets were filled with a throng of merry pleasure drivers, and the scene was much the same, excepting the fact that the jam was much greater. A number of very fine turnouts made their appearance during the afternoon, and probably the one of these which attracted the most attention was the "rig" of Mr. Joel Thomas, driven tandem, and which was acknowledged to be "the boss of the road." The unusual fall of snow has given an opportunity seldom enjoyed in this city, and the number and variety in style of the extemporized cutters is something amazing.
December 17

A Slice of the TIMES

-The shock of the fall of the Frank's Hall building was felt three blocks away, and the crash was heard in West Kansas.
December 19

-Photographs of the ruins of Frank's Hall were yesterday taken and reproduced upon the canvass of the Comique last night.
December 19
The weight of what was said to have been the heaviest snowfall in years finally proved to be too much for the roof of Frank's Hall, on the corner of Fifth and Main, and it fell in on December 18. Luckily the building was unoccupied, and no one was hurt.

-Manager Love, of the Theatre Comique, had the roof of his building thoroughly cleaned, directly after the late storm, and there is no danger of its falling.
December 19

-A section of the north wall of Frank's Hall fell a little after noon yesterday, while the workmen engaged in the work of tearing down the building were at dinner. No harm was done, but the crash drew a large crowd into the street and caused quite an excitement for a few minutes.
December 21

-The Mayor yesterday received several additional contributions, in the way of sacks of flour, etc., to the Christmas dinner for the poor.
December 22

A Test of Temperance - 1878

-And Cosby the ex-news agent now sleeps happy. He has just had the patent burglar alarm put up in his house, which, if touched, not only alarms him but the whole neighborhood.
December 22

-There was trouble in the ice business yesterday, the men with teams striking, demanding $3 per day or 25 cents a load. Matters therefore were quiet yesterday morning, but towards afternoon a compromise was effected and they went to work at 20 cents per load.
December 24

-Already the work upon Frank's Hall has been so far advanced that a temporary roof is nearly completed and the building will soon be again ready for occupancy. That it is now perfectly safe, no one doubts, and the location in which it stands will probably give a full list of tenants at once.
December 24

-Not a child's sleigh could be found in the city yesterday, all being sold out. One dealer stated he had sold 300 within the past ten days.
December 25

-Jake Arnsden, who works for Plankington & Armour, got his ear frozen yesterday, and not thinking, pinched it, taking a piece completely out of his ear, it being rendered so brittle by the frost.
December 25

A Slice of the TIMES

-The sale of dry goods was suspended Christmas. The sale of "wet" goods, however, went on with increased activity.
December 28

-Nothing but encomiums for Mr. Shelley are heard whenever the Mayor's connection with the late Christmas dinner for the poor is mentioned.
December 28

-If there is any law to enforce those driving in cutters or sleighs to carry bells on their horses, it should be carried out. Yesterday a horse drawing a light cutter without any bells came nearly running over three little boys on Ninth street, West Kansas. The rig making no noise was upon them before they were aware of their danger.
December 28

-An old negro who has been complained of for "keeping a boarding house," he says, and whose case is in the hands of Prosecuting Attorney Peak, was about the Court House all day yesterday. He is 108 years old, and came to Missouri in 1822. His name is John Rice, and his recollections of the early days, as yesterday related, are found to be of great interest, and are fully corroborated by old residents.
December 31

-1878, can not survive twenty-four hours. The best physicians in the town have given up the case as hopeless.
December 31

All the Sanitary Measures
1879

In 1879, after years of experimentation, Thomas A. Edison finally found a material that would burn for 45 hours without overheating, and the electric light was born. A short time later he settled on carbonized bamboo, which could burn for 1,000 hours. New York saw wide use of Edison's new light source in 1882, while Kansas City had carbon arc electric street lights (an earlier, less appealing invention) in 1881.

The Yellow Fever epidemic in the South the previous year may have been the wake-up call that Kansas Citians needed to begin the vital efforts to clean up their town. Mayor Shelley led the way by forming the first Board of Health. They began swiftly to eliminate the "pestial nuisances" found throughout the city.

A Slice of the TIMES

-The thermometer at Plankington & Armour's fell to 12 below zero yesterday at noon, and it was stated where they were cutting ice it got down to 20 below. However, be that as it may, all hands declared it too cold to work, and quit accordingly.
January 3

-Pretty cold in West Kansas on Thursday night - the whiskey even froze in some of the saloons.
January 4

-A person may have too much of a good thing, even if it is a bountiful supply of water. Dr. Horton thought so early yesterday morning when having to get out about 2 o'clock and hunt up the waterworks man and stop the flow of water at his house. One of the pipes breaking from the front flooded everything in a few moments. The damage was repaired as soon as possible, and the doctor can once more sleep in peace.
January 9

-The coasting in various portions of the city was never better than at the present time, and nightly the various eligible hills are besieged with crowds of people out enjoying the exhilarating sport. Last night Tenth, Jefferson, from Tenth down to Ninth, and Penn streets were the favorite localities, and until a late hour were they taken possession of by the warmly-clad, enjoyment-loving pleasure-seekers. On the Tenth street hill quite an accident

occurred, Mr. Apperson receiving a severe injury to his knees, though it is hoped nothing serious will result.
January 18

-Plankinton & Armour have now got 22,000 tons of ice at their establishment.
January 19

-A. S. Orbison is now running 75 teams and 135 men at his ice runway. He has got out thus far 33,000 tons of ice.
January 19

-A. S. Orbison closed his ice business for the season yesterday, he having got out over 45,000 tons.
January 23

-A pair of boy's boots in an inverted position are just visible over a pond at the corner of second and Walnut streets, and the sign "Danger!" close at hand. Very suggestive at this time.
January 23

-The colored cornet band of Lexington made music in the air at Long's Hall yesterday, and at night held a festival at the same place.
March 19

A Slice of the TIMES

-The subscription list for the Telephone Exchange is being circulated. Every one should make up their minds and give it their support without hesitation, as it is undoubtedly, an institution that is much needed in this city, and no one will regret having connected themselves with it. All the principal connections have been secured and all that is wanting now is to complete the list so that the work of putting up the wires and instruments can be commenced. It will take three or four weeks to make all the connections after the list is complete. A contract for one year only is asked, and the subscribers can then use their pleasure about renewing: The list should be filled at once.
March 19

-Mr. John Branham, the enterprising proprietor of the Liverpool meat market, went home to dinner yesterday to be greeted by an infant daughter, kicking the beam at 10 pounds. The smile that stole over his good looking face held its own all day, and at night changed to a broad grin of satisfaction. He was the happiest man in town.
March 20

-A large party of Kaw Indians arrived in West Kansas yesterday in full war paint, feathers, etc. They were however pretty peaceable, and punished nothing except some fire water.
March 28

184

-Sturgeon, the man living in "Hell's Half Acre" who attempted suicide Sunday night, yesterday refused to take any medicine, or, in fact, anything whatever. He, therefore, stands an excellent chance of giving the undertaker a job yet.
April 2

-The Union Depot presents a busy sight as the trains roll in, bearing their living cargoes bound for all points of the compass. The emigrant seeking a new home in the West; the health-seeker bound for Colorado to recuperate his shattered strength; the commercial man, at home in all places - a very cosmopolite; and the restless tourist, never satisfied but ever longing for new scenes to visit.
April 2

-Mr. M. D. Wood, General Manager of the Telephone Exchange, has put a large force of men to work running wires for the Telephone Exchange, and will soon have the entire circuit completed, which will be equipped with Edison's improved telephones, and strictly first-class in every respect.
April 4

-A young man from Lawrence made complaint at police headquarters yesterday that he had been roped into a saloon on Main street, and beaten out of his watch and chain and sixty dollars in money. The fellow came to town to see the sights, and was "collared" by "the gang," and fleeced in less than no time.
April 5

A Slice of the TIMES

-Don't trade any votes to-day but take the whole ticket straight.
April 8

-Don't leave the polls till you vote for Chace, Craig and Yeager.
April 8

-Vote for John Salisbury in the Fourth ward and for Hickey in the sixth.
April 8

-Sturgeon, the man who poisoned himself has recovered, and is ready for another dose - furnish more items for West Kansas.
April 8

-The election passed off quietly and orderly, hardly any drunkenness or disorder being manifested.
April 9

-Farewell the glowing speech, the effusive candidate, the bonfire, the brass band. Farewell, a farewell for one short year.
April 9

-The old buildings at the corner of Main and Sixth streets are being demolished to make way for a fine three-story brick structure to be used by the well-known furniture warehouse of Abernathy, North & Orrison. W. C. Lobenstein is to erect the new

building, and it will be ready for occupancy by Aug. 1.
April 9

-"Paddy" Joyce, a notorious hoodlum about town, was arrested yesterday by one of Marshal Ligget's deputies, charged with disturbing the peace. Joyce is one of the worst young rascals in the city, and on Thursday night of last week went down to the east levee and raised cain generally and succeeded in partially breaking up the services in the Holmes street Mission. A warrant was at once sworn out for his arrest, but he kept in the dark until yesterday. He will have a hearing to-day.
April 19

-The Joe Kinney is expected to arrive to-day or to-morrow. It is impossible to state which, owing to the shallowness of the river.
April 24

-At Lawrence, Kansas, the dusky negroes are taking possession of the city by storm. A few nights ago, it was reported impossible to walk any distance at all without stepping upon the negroes, who had, through necessity, taken the ground for a couch, and the blue canopy of heaven for a coverlet.
April 24

-The Council should, at its session to-night, take up and pass the Board of Health bill, which is now ready, having been thoroughly overhauled by a

187

A Slice of the TIMES

committee consisting of nearly every physician in town. By the provisions of the bill the Mayor is President of the Board, and it should be passed at once and steps taken to provide for the hot weather, which is sure to come.

April 25

-Probably one of the most remarkable instances of the strange freaks which nature occasionally indulges in is now on exhibition at Turner Hall. It is a live headless chicken. A reporter of the TIMES last evening interviewed the owner and gleaned from him the following facts: On Saturday last L. A. C. Uhlman, proprietor of an eating house at Joplin, Mo., killed in all about a dozen chickens. When to his surprise this one, which is a species of the Black Spanish tribe, commenced walking about after its head had been completely severed from its body. This so excited Mr. Uhlman's curiosity that he immediately caught the chicken and applied the proper remedies to prevent it from bleeding to death. Since then he has fed and watered it with a small silver tube regularly three times a day, and last evening it appeared as lively as though nothing had occurred. He has its head carefully preserved, so there can possibly be no deception. To-day and to-morrow it will be on exhibition at Turner Hall, and it is well worth anyone's time to see a remarkably singular occurrence, one that very seldom occurs, if at all, in one's life time.

April 25

-Yesterday was the last day that dogs could run without the required licensing.
April 26

-Manager Wood, of the Gold and Stock Telephone Exchange, has decided to make a sweeping reduction of rates and to put in operation at once the system under contemplation by that company for some time. Mr. Wood proposes to furnish his patrons first-class instruments and at as low prices as any other company. This insures the permanent success of a worthy enterprise.
April 26

-For some days past there has been considerable talk between two gentlemen, each of whom claimed to possess the swiftest roadster, and finally it culminated in a match of $100 a side, which took place at the Exposition grounds. Joe Loeffer enters bay filly Lucy L. Frank Kump enters bay mare Fergy. With light scoring they got a good send off, and Fergy proved an easy winner in two straight heats. Time, 3:15. The race was the subject of much interest and a great deal of comment.
April 29

-The Telephone Exchange Company on yesterday connected the offices of the Chief of Police and that of the Fire Department with one of their instruments. To-day they will make the connection of the office of the Chief Police and that of the County Marshal.
May 1

A Slice of the TIMES

-After to-day it is hoped the horde of hotel runners, who infest the approach to the Union Depot, will be considerably lessened, as the license is now $100 instead of $10. The up town and first class hotels will, of course, have representatives at the depot, as is right, but the mob of boys and loafers who yell and haul at passengers as they come from the trains, can be spared and never missed.
May 1

-The telephone at the police headquarters proved to be a novelty and quite an attraction to many of the casual visitors to that place yesterday.
May 2

-Officer Schrumpf was made the recipient of a handsome silver plated dog collar by Geo. Hale on yesterday. It bore the following inscription: "I am officer Schrumpf's dog, who are you?"
May 2

-The independent indifference of many who are out work is astonishing. A TIMES' reporter on questioning a gang lazily sitting in the shade, found that out of ten or a dozen ablebodied men, only two were willing to work for less than $1.50 per day. The rest remarked, "we will beg first." They all, however, joined in one voice in praising the citizens generally of this city for their liberality in feeding the nomadic tribe.
May 3

All the Sanitary Measures - 1879

-There are now 118 houses in process of erection in West Kansas.
May 4

-The row of cottages being put up by Jerome, on Mulberry street, West Kansas, are progressing at the rate of one a day. The contractor commenced Friday morning and had two completed by last evening. The whole twenty-five will be built and ready for use in almost thirty days.
May 4

-Telephones are in active operations in the Merchant's Exchange, and the constant calling keeps up a succession of sweet sounds.
May 4

-The corps of U. S. Enginerrs now in the city are busily engaged in getting ready to expend that $30,000 appropriated to improve the river in this neighborhood. Work will be commenced to-day on the scows which are to be built here, and which it will be necessary to have in order to properly prosecute the work.
May 7

-The work of filling the various ponds and mud holes in different parts of the city is progressing rapidly, and soon they will be a remembrance of the past.
May 8

-Residences in various parts of the city are being painted, which is beautifying their appearance greatly. The prevailing color for brick houses is a light drab, with dark trimmings and green blinds, while for frame ones the old stand-by, white, is being extensively used.
May 8

-The daily activity apparent on the market square shows what a large extent of country regards Kansas City as the only place to dispose of their produce.
May 10

-Jack Gallagher, the dog-catcher, will commence his work of destruction on Monday, and desires all persons owning dogs to have them licensed immediately or they will be taken up next week, as sure as his name is Gallagher.
May 10

-If you miss your pet dog, hurry to the pound at the foot of Main street and secure a license, and then Jack Gallagher will turn over the animal.
May 15

-The upper portion of the Union Depot is being finished off into rooms for the use of travelers. Mr. Blossom, at the depot, is to have charge of the new quarters.
May 15

-Runaways are of almost daily occurrence. Owners of horses should be compelled to hitch their horses when left alone.
May 15

-Over seven hundred building permits have been issued during the present year.
May 15

-Between forty-five and fifty dogs were annihilated by Jack Gallagher yesterday.
May 17

-The proposed improvement of the Independence road will make that the most fashionable drive.
May 17

-Kansas City, which has for so long had a sort of "out-at-elbows" appearance in places, promises to be soon as solidly built up as could be wished.
May 17

-A colored man, stating that he was a Senator from Mississippi, who came up on the Kate Kinney, was around in West Kansas yesterday soliciting funds to help the colored people now camped near elevator "A." He complained that the committee had done nothing for them, and that they were sick, hungry, and destitute.
May 17
The Senator's name was Blanche Kelso Bruce. He was sworn in on March 5, 1875.

A Slice of the TIMES

-Over one hundred canines have been put to death by the dog catcher during the past week.
May 20

-On Thursday next there will be a strawberry festival and hop at the Trabue House, West Kansas.
May 20

-Last night the TIMES office was placed in communication with the central office of the Kansas City Telephone Company, and in a few days will be able to converse with all points of interest throughout the city by telephone. The switch board arrived yesterday and this company in a short time will have everything in apple pie order.
May 20

-Jack Gallagher's trade is decreasing, unlicensed canines being difficult to find.
May 22

-The Gold and Stock Telephone Exchange answered over four hundred and seventy calls during business hours yesterday. No better evidence of prosperity in business circles could be calculated.
May 22

-Jack Gallagher has completely cleaned out the curs in West Kansas, few being seen now-a-days.
May 25

-An interesting walking contest will take place at the Tivoli Garden on Sunday afternoon, between William West and John Oddy, for a purse of $20. Both are excellent pedestrians, and those who attend may expect to see the distance, 25 miles, covered in fast time.
May 30

-As an evidence of the great amount of business transacted at the office of the Gold and Stock Telephone Exchange, it can be stated that over one thousand calls were answered yesterday, the majority of them being from business houses.
June 4

-The statement in Tuesday's TIMES that the steamer Ashland ran aground near Plankinton & Armours, while coming down the river, was a mistake. She stopped there awhile on account of the high wind, and then passed through the draw-bridge in safety.
June 4

-The Bell Telephone Company, with office over the Bank of Kansas City, will before long have one of their instruments in the Theatre Comique. This will permit business men, their wives and children to hear the orchestra and other sweet sounds from the Comique without going out in the cold - or rather warm weather.
June 5

A Slice of the TIMES

-A pet antelope was one of the curiosities at the Union Depot yesterday.
June 11

-Jack Gallagher with his crew gathered up quite a drove of stray hogs in West Kansas yesterday.
June 11

-Last night a large number of the patrons of the Bell Telephone Company were connected with the Theatre Comique wire, and during the whole evening were in communication with that place of amusement. It was quite a novelty to sit in one's house or office and hear the orchestra at the Comique playing different tunes, as it also was to hear the various solos and duets sung upon the stage. All the music comes through use of the small microphones in use by the Bell Company.
June 12

-The Mayor has issued a proclamation calling attention to the matter of depositing garbage and refuse in the streets.
June 13

-The Board of Health is now fully organized, and yesterday efforts were about the streets notifying owners of smelling sewers and closets that the same must be abated at once.
June 13

All the Sanitary Measures - 1879

-The Waterworks Company on Sunday cleaned the upper reservoir. The water was let out and the work thoroughly performed. The Superintendent says that there was but little sediment found, and that the reservoir was in better condition than the Company had anticipated. It was owing to this cleaning, the Superintendent says, that the Kaw water was yesterday so milky in appearance.
July 1

-Take up your wooden sidewalks and build anew before the 20th of July, or the city will do it for you.
July 3

-Chief of Fire Department Foster yesterday had an engine all day employed in the work of draining the pond at the southeast corner of Sixth and Central streets. The residents in that vicinity will be a grateful people if the work is continued until the pond is emptied.
July 4

-The two "favorite" ball nines of the city, the "Kansas City Red Stockings" and the "Kansas City Browns," are now in excellent trim, fully uniformed and equipped, and will play their first match at the Riverview Park, where the Browns have laid out a fine diamond, on Saturday afternoon. Go and see the willow weilders. No extra admission fee for carriages.
July 9

A Slice of the TIMES

-The mounted police made their first appearance in West Kansas yesterday afternoon.
July 9

-Seven burial permits were issued yesterday from the Board of Health office. There has been a rapid increase of mortality among the infant population during the past week of hot weather.
July 9

-General George C. Bingham's funeral services will be conducted at the late residence of the deceased at ten o'clock this morning. The remains will be interred in the Union Cemetery.
July 9

-A system of district sewerage for the city is now the subject of consideration by the city engineer. Elaborate plans may be now seen at his office in the City Hall of the district embraced by Walnut, McGee, Thirteenth, and Sixteenth streets. It is proposed to provide district pipes, which will empty into the Walnut street main. The residents of Grand avenue and McGee streets have been petitioning for sewerage facilities, and will feel gratified that there is something being done in the matter.
July 22

-The pool of stagnant water know as Sheridan's pond, opposite the Metropolitan Hotel, is to be drained. The contract is let and Monday the syphon will commence pumping the basin dry.
August 1

-The West Kansas drinking fountains were put in yesterday, and will be well patronized by temperance people.
August 3

-The new Board of Health say they intend to "make things hump."
August 9

-In various portions of the city garbage in the streets awaits the scavengers' call, and the new Board of Health assistant sanitary superintendent should be up and doing.
August 9

-Ed Kelley, of the Mechanics' Hotel, is putting in drain pipe all around and under his hotel in West Kansas, bound to use all the sanitary measures in his power to keep health.
August 9

-The B. of H. is actively at work. The president rather depreciates the idea that the city is usually unclean, and says that it was never cleaner. The board has plenty of authority, and whenever it once cleanses things it intends to make property-holders keep them in proper condition.
August 12

A Slice of the TIMES

-The ordinances require the hacks to stand in one place on Main street. They also will not permit two to stand abreast, and there are so many hacks that all of them cannot stand in line. "What is a fellow going to do, you know?" the hackmen ask.
August 15

-The remains of an old land mark - the ancient elm tree at the corner of Main street and Ninth, was dragged from its long resting place yesterday by a team of horses. The removal was witnessed by a crowd of at least one hundred persons, and the stump and projecting roots were quickly scattered by the mob.
August 15

-At the pound there are now 52 dogs, 8 cows and a pair of high-stepping horses. Gallagher killed 22 dogs on Friday, and will make another slaughter of the innocents to-day. Jack says he is now attending strictly to business, and will keep his pound full as long as there is an estray about the city.
August 17

-An old colored woman attracted much attention at the depot yesterday, with her luggage and little ones. She stated, "Ise gwine back to da Mississip'. Kansas am no place for de colored folks."
August 19

-The City Hospital is crowded with patients, and Dr. Porter says new quarters will have to be provided for future cases of destitution.
August 21

-There is a project on foot in West Kansas to start "a railroad man's hospital." A meeting of the leading citizens will take place next week, in West Kansas, to decide on location and provide for the raising of the necessary funds.
August 21

-The water in the Missouri river is lower.
August 26

-The river is so low that no water is now running through the slough, and the sand bar reaches to the Harlem bank.
August 26

-The syphon is still at work on Sheridan pond, and the old water-make is already several feet above the present level of the pond.
August 26

-The rear wall of the partially completed building on Fifth street west of Broadway, was demolished yesterday by the caving in of a high bank of clay.
August 26

A Slice of the TIMES

-It is estimated that the number of crooked men in town is over 200, all sneak thieves, pickpockets and burglars. Their operations have been heretofore confined to the Fair and Union depot, but during to-day and to-morrow some big schemes will probably be hatched out just as the gangs intend leaving.
August 26

-To-day the dog-catcher performs the last rites for twenty-seven unclaimed canines. There will also be a sale of twenty-two ownerless swine.
August 27

-Jack Gallagher and party arrived in the "Patch" West Kansas, last evening, and commenced operations, but the first yell given by a captured dog brought out the inhabitants of the "Patch" entire. Stones and rocks fell like hail, and windows were mashed in all directions. Jack and his crew were forced to retreat after having captured one yaller dog.
September 3

-A number of Kansas City young people left yesterday to attend the college at St. Mary's, Kas., which opened on Tuesday.
September 4

-The draining of the Sheridan pond is almost accomplished. The siphon still pursues its quiet but effective work, and but a small area of water remains in the hollow once nearly filled by the

pond. The removal of this great nuisance has been performed at small cost, and if the draining of the other Central street ponds can be effected in the same manner the accomplishment of a good work, well done, will be properly credited by the public.
September 4

-School children could be seen yesterday in all directions, with books and baskets, on their way to the various departments of learning.
September 9

-A swarm of candidates for positions on the police force and witnesses in cases before the Police Commissioners, gathered about the Court House last evening and made a lively scene.
October 29

-All the hotels are crowded with guests and still the boom continues.
October 31

-The wise turkey counts the days to Thanksgiving and abstains from hearty eating.
October 31

-A very bright looking little boy about 6 years old came into the Kansas Pacific Land Office, yesterday afternoon, and asked for the General Superintendent. He stated his name was Lampher, and that he was staying with his mother, who drank up all he earned and left him to take care of himself,

A Slice of the TIMES

and that his father was working in Denver, and he wanted to get a pass to that point. The address of S. Smith was given him and he went his way, but with what success he met with was not learned.
November 1

-The Council last night was the scene of a discussion relating to Jack Gallagher, the City Impounder, in which it was stated that his fees were so large as to cover the amounts received from the sale of stock. The numerous complaints of the actions of Jack's men will cause an investigation to be made at an early day in the shape, probably, of a charge against him in the Council of malfeasance.
November 4

-Nineteen able bodied men stood in the rain yesterday for an hour, watching a man paint a sign on Fifth and Main streets.
November 11

-The undertakers were unusually busy yesterday, there being over a dozen burials outside of the victims of the fire.
November 11
The fire occurred on Friday, November 7, in Corles' factory, 206 Main street. A cooking starch explosion caused the collapse of the upper floors of that building, and attached buildings 204 and 208 Main. The fire resulted in the deaths of at least six people.

-Workmen were busy removing brick and debris from the ruins of last Friday.
November 13

All the Sanitary Measures - 1879

-Death has been busy of late in the household of Mr. John Farrel, who has charge of the County Jail. A week age a beloved boy was smitten by the hand of death, and last night his little Ella, five years of age, closed her eyes in the sleep of death. Much sympathy is felt for Mr. Farrel in this heavy affliction. The remains of Ella will be taken to-day to Independence for burial.
November 14

-A new patent car coupler drew quite a crowd of railway men at the depot yesterday.
November 15

-Notwithstanding the tirade made against dogs during the past year, only 504 have been registered up to date.
November 15

-The notorious Morman Ann was arrested at 1 o'clock this morning for perambulating the streets without an escort.
November 22

-A number of men are hard at work trying to save some portion of the bridge span that went tumbling into the Kaw river last Wednesday night.
November 22

-Plankinton & Armour now have nearly eight hundred hands employed at their institution.
November 27

A Slice of the TIMES

-Plankinton & Armour are going to do away with the old hand method of scraping hogs, and the beginning of next week the hair will be removed from the animal by a steam apparatus.
November 27

-A report will be prepared from the City Engineer's office showing, among other facts, the number of buildings erected the present year and the cost. It is estimated the figures will reach nearly nine hundred thousand dollars.
December 5

-It is stated on good authority that if the present weather continues a special levy will be made and signs with "No bottom" painted on them placed at the principal crossings for the better guidance of passers by.
December 6

-Annie Porter, the crippled colored woman, who came here with the refugees and journeyed around the country an outcast, returned to Kansas City and was sent to the hospital by Mayor Shelley yesterday. Topeka and Sedalia turned her out to die, and although she has no claim on Kansas City, she will be taken care of.
December 10

All the Sanitary Measures - 1879

-The wording of the questions on death certificates are a puzzle to physicians. One question is "civil condition?" meaning married or single. To this query the Board of Health has received some novel answers, such as "carpenter," "Baptist," One physician certified that the civil condition of the corpse was "good."
December 12

-Skating is rapidly becoming a popular pastime and should the weather continue cold the ponds would soon be covered by gay crowds seeking healthful recreation.
December 18

-One hundred and fifty refugees arrived yesterday, bag and baggage. They were a pitiful sight as they stood shivering in the cold. They left last night for Topeka, and it is to be hoped that Governor St. John will kindly care for the future voters.
December 19

-The Union Depot looked like an uptown toy shop yesterday, so many people being there with Christmas presents on their way home.
December 24

-As this New Year's day will come in Leap Year, the young men in the court house, propose to keep open house, and have the ladies visit them, instead of going out on the war path as usual.
December 30

"Exodusters"
1880

During the summer of 1879, African Americans began to leave Mississippi in great numbers for Kansas and other points west. Motivated by increasingly intolerable conditions in Mississippi and inflated claims of wealth and prosperity to be had in Kansas, 20,000 - 40,000 people began a disorganized and dangerous journey west. Kansas, a poor state at the time, did what she could to provide for the "Exodusters" (so named because of their exodus to the dusty plains of Kansas). Many were unable to complete the trip and were forced to remain wherever their money ran out. Their great numbers and desperate plight were not recognized in Kansas City until 1880, where their journey was reaching its end.

1880 was also another Presidential Election year, and this time things proceeded more smoothly, but were not without controversy. After ugly, personal campaigning on both sides, James A. Garfield, Republican, was elected president. He won by less than 2,000 votes. Eight months later, in July of 1881, Garfield was shot in the back and killed by Charles Guiteau, who wanted to see Vice President Chester A. Arthur become President. Guiteau was hanged for the crime June 30, 1882.

1880 brought a new evening newspaper to Kansas City. Begun by William Rockhill Nelson on September 18, 1880, the Kansas City STAR brought stiff competition to the TIMES and others from the very first day. In 1901 the STAR dominated the newspaper business in Kansas City to such an extent that it bought out the TIMES and kept it as its morning paper.

"Exodusters" - 1880

-The New Year was welcomed in last night in good old fashioned style, with the exception of the chimes. The gay revellers thronged the streets and made night merry with the crack of harmless pistol shots and the noise of fire crackers. In several parts of the city fireworks were displayed, making a beautiful picture in the frozen sky. Something less than a million of people swore off several million bad habits, and the new cycle was ushered in with great joy and thanksgiving.
January 1

-The TIMES force have sworn off to a man - don't tempt them!
January 1

-A slippery place in crossing Main and Eighth streets yesterday caused a number of bad falls. A large crowd gathered and enjoyed the unusual display of striped hosiery. Pedestrians soon tumbled to the racket.
January 1

-The pedestrians on Main street were paralyzed yesterday by the appearance of a sweep on the crossings. The sweep is a colored boy and is said to have made quite a sum of money from grateful pedestrians. It would be an excellent idea for some of the bootblacks and news boys to work on the crossings. It would be profitable and much easier than their present work.
January 4

A Slice of the TIMES

-Some alarm has been caused in the last week by the breaking out in several localities of the dreaded scourge, measles.
January 6

-The crossings of the streets in West Kansas are in deplorable condition. Before anything serious occurs they should be put into shape.
January 6

-F. Dorkins, a colored man, was at the Union Depot yesterday complaining bitterly how they had been deceived in coming to Kansas. He was from Winsted, Miss., and owned 100 acres of land there. He said all colored people were well off there, but nearly 800 in Topeka alone were starving, besides hundreds at other points in the far West.
January 6

-Six families of exodusters came in on the North Missouri yesterday.
January 8

-Over the muddy crossing
   Trips a maid with eyes of blue,
Daintly lifting her dress skirt
   Above a buttoned shoe.

In a neighboring window
   Sits a wicked, wicked man,
He's looking at that girl's ankle
   As hard as he ever can.

Summer will come, with all its roses
And sweetly smelling hay,
But for seeing striped stockings
There's no time like to-day.
January 8

-A drunken man trying to take home a more
drunken woman, was one of the disgusting sights on
Santa Fe street, yesterday morning.
January 10

-A Leavenworth maiden in love
Put some kerosene oil in the stove.
It is thought that her toes
Were turned up as she rose,
By the size of the hole just above.
January 10

-The contract for grading Tracy avenue between
Ninth and Tenth street has been awarded to James
Dehoney at twenty-three cents per yard. The
contracts for building sidewalks were let at thirty-
eight cents per foot.
January 11

-On Monday, if the weather permits, City Engineer
Knickerbocker will start his force to work cleaning
the principal business streets. The mud will be
scraped together and carted away instead of being
washed off, as resolved by the City Council. With
the work well done, the city will next be placed in
good condition for the next storm.
January 11

A Slice of the TIMES

-Highway robbery has become an epidemic and no less than five cases were reported yesterday.
January 17

-Nine families of exodusters came in yesterday. They went to Topeka.
January 23

-Quoits is now the leading game among the business men in West Kansas.
January 23

-From the number of robberies, safe blowings, burglaries, etc., committed during the week, it is evident that a gang of thieves are at work in the city. The work is done by professionals who are well up in the business.
January 24

-One hundred and twenty-two "badly busted" exodusters came in on the North Missouri yesterday. They having no funds to get any further, destitution threatens over the bottoms in West Kansas.
January 27

-The probabilities are that no more street crossings will be laid or repaired for the remainder of the fiscal year for want of funds.
February 6

"Exodusters" - 1880

-Each fire plug in the city costs taxpayers eighty-five dollars a year. The city's bill for water is nearly $37,000 per annum at present and will reach $40,000 next year.
February 7

-The death rate in Kansas City is a little over fourteen per cent, including deaths from accidents, which ought not to effect the health showing. In comparison with other cities it places Kansas City away up on the list.
February 7

-West Kansas is getting alarmed at the number of Exodusters that keep pouring in daily.
February 8

-Down on the river bank yesterday fourteen homeless curs were slaughtered by the dog catcher, Jack Gallagher.
February 11

-A necessity exists for a telephone to the City Hospital and it is understood that the Council will be requested to have one placed there immediately.
February 13

-The gas at the depot suddenly failed on Wednesday night and left the platform in darkness from seven until nine o'clock, during which time the pickpockets raided the crowd and reaped a harvest.
February 13

A Slice of the TIMES

-Two hundred exodusters passed through to Topeka on Saturday.
February 24

-A well known firm in West Kansas bought a double barrelled shot-gun a few days since to keep off robbers, and placed the same in their office. Yesterday one of the aforesaid robbers came along and carried off the weapon.
February 24

-Casper Widmer, a grocery man, threw high dice at George Miller's saloon on Union avenue last night and won a horse, buggy and harness, valued at $200, put up by Jno. Rogers.
February 26

-The Bell Telephone Company intend introducing a new system by which wires will be run taking in twenty-five offices each and so arranged that any number can be connected at once. Connection can thus be made immediately by simply pushing a button and giving two numbers, a boy listening for signals constantly.
February 26

-Another installment of 220 exodusters arrived yesterday morning on the North Missouri.
March 3

-The building permits issued from January 1 up to yesterday footed up $255,000 with a rising ground-swell.
March 3

-Before all of the sidewalk on Mulberry street between Eleventh and Twelfth streets is stolen it should be relaid.
March 4

O'er the puzzle Brown is bending,
 Never once his strained eyes liftin'-
See! He thinks at last he's triumphed;
 No! 'tis 14 -- 13 -- 15.

Once again he tries the puzzle,
 Puzzle that there's fatal sport in;
Ha! He's got it now! Not much he
 Hasn't, 13 -- 15 -- 14.

Long he pauses, long he ponders,
 Now he thinks he's got it certain,
Moves the figures very slowly -
 Pshaw! 'tis 15 -- 14 -- 13.

See! his eyes dilate and glisten!
 Into madness he is a driftin'!
One more victim for the asylum,
 Crazed by 13 -- 14 -- 15.
March 7
The puzzle, 13 - 14 - 15, consisted of a small wooden frame containing 15 small blocks, with spaces for 16 blocks. The 15

blocks were numbered 1 through 15 and the object of the puzzle was to slide the blocks, one at a time using the one empty space, into numerical order. You can still find these today.

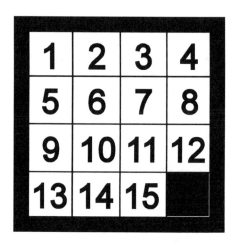

-The fifteen puzzle craze has struck the Merchant's Exchange building with fatal effect. The boys at Schroeder's spend hours trying to make 13, 14, 15 come out correct.
March 9

-The whole city has a violent attack of the 13, 15, 14 craze.
March 10

-"I made it once, but I can't do it again."
March 11

-Even Sam Ralls is getting daft on 13, 15, 14, and takes the puzzle to bed with him.
March 11

"Exodusters" - 1880

-Every man who lives on Thirteenth, Fourteenth, or Fifteenth streets has got it bad.
March 11

-Sheriff Bailey was obliged to hire a small boy to serve papers yesterday, all the deputies being engaged on 14, 13, 15.
March 11

-Johnny Campbell says it can't be done. He will be out in a few days.
March 11

-Fifty-five exodusters from Grenada County, Miss., arrived yesterday and went to Topeka.
March 12

-The TIMES will present a silver mine, and $15 in money, to any one who will solve that everlasting 13, 15, 14 matter, and tell how it is done.
March 12

-The 13 - 14 - 15 puzzle case struck the City Treasurer's office yesterday, and Vincent and Walmsley wore out the skin on their right forefinger trying to make the thing jibe.
March 12

-Two hundred and twenty-five more exodusters arrived yesterday.
March 18

-Don't forget the Democratic Primaries to-night.
March 26

A Slice of the TIMES

-Be sure that you are registered. The registrars are at the old Court House, and if you were out of town last week, go now and have your names placed on the books.
March 26

-The TIMES published an April Fool sensation yesterday on the 14 - 15 puzzle which was justly appreciated by the large crowd which called at the station.
April 2
The TIMES ran an "interview" with a fictitious fifteen year old boy who said he could solve the 14 -15 puzzle every time, and offered to show anyone how to do it if they met him at the Depot before his train departed.

-As can be seen by reference to the report of the School Board meeting held last evening there are now within the limits of Kansas City 15,275 school children. This is an increase of 3,950 over last year, and at the regular ratio gives a population of 61,600. The enumeration of the school children can be relied upon, having been in the hands of a most capable man.
April 2

-Nearly three hundred exodusters came in yesterday morning.
April 4

-A child was left on the steps of the Women's Christian Home on Friday night.
April 4

-The steamer Fannie Lewis left a large delegation of exodusters in West Kansas, Sunday night. There were in quite destitute condition.
April 6

-A small safe in the office of the Diamond Mills in West Kansas was blown open Monday night, but the safe-blower found only twenty cents. There is supposed to be a gang of safe burglars in town.
April 7

-The baby left on the steps of the Women's Christian Home is ready for adoption.
April 9

-A large number of the lately arrived exodusters are sleeping out in the open air in "Hell's Half Acre," with all their worldly goods beside them.
April 9

-Jack Gallagher says he intends to resign his position as Public Impounder.
April 13

-For the first time in this month, no exodusters arrived yesterday.
April 14

-Jack Gallagher says he has made a complete and full report of his stewardship to the City Clerk, and that the loss of his books by the late fire falls only

upon his shoulders.
April 16
The fire, a few days earlier, resulted from a lamp apparently knocked over by one of the animals in the pound. The pound buildings, all wood frame and cheaply built, were completely destroyed, but only two dogs were killed.

-There will be a boulevard meeting at the Coates' House at 8 o'clock this evening of those interested in the Rosedale project.
April 21
This project resulted in Southwest Boulevard, the first "named" boulevard in Kansas City.

-Four dollars per month is asked by the ice dealers for fifteen pounds of ice daily. How poor mortals will have to sweat this summer.
April 23

-The Market House is to be repaired, and its stall capacity enlarged.
May 4

-Gas will be furnished to the city at $22 per post, instead of $28 as heretofore.
May 4

-Jack Gallager's report to the Council was immense. He says he cannot live at the price paid.
May 4

-Eighty-five families of exodusters came in yesterday over the North Missouri. They went out on the Fort Scott Road bound for the coal mines at Coffee County.
May 7

-Jack Gallagher is happy over his appointment as a salaried officer. He says he will give the reporters something to talk about before long.
May 7

-Census Supervisor Duke has made his appointments, a full list of which will appear to-morrow. There are 265 41 men, and Kansas City 21 men.
May 14

-It was so hot yesterday that it melted the pitch off the roof of the building on the northeast corner of Main street and Missouri avenue to such an extent that the sticky stuff ran down the gutter onto the sidewalk.
May 14

-The Brown Stocking Base Ball Club (colored), gave an anniversary festival at Long's Hall last night.
May 15

-The new ordinances governing hotel and ticket runners makes it a misdemeanor for them to solicit on the depot platform or any walk leading thereto,

or upon any sidewalk on Union avenue. This leaves
them to solicit in the street only, which will be very
unpleasant on rainy days. The ordinance also stops
the hideous gang in the Union Depot.
May 19

-Old Uncle Wash Dale, ninety-four years of age
and a resident of this district for seventy-four years,
intends applying for admission to the Old Settlers
Association. He is the boss old settler.
May 20

-The Union Depot Hotel on Union avenue, evades
the ordinance by having their runners stand at an
upstairs window and yell out the merits of the
house.
May 20

-Since April 20, Assistant Sanitary Superintendent
Wilson has abated 100 out of 118 nuisances
reported.
May 25

-Plankinton & Armour ship weekly nearly a
quarter of a million pounds of material from their
fertilizing establishment.
May 29

-The peanut venders and stand keepers succeeded
in passing an ordinance last night allowing stands
on streets running east and west.
May 29

-Travelers have a new dodge now. They carry a small chain and padlock and when in the waiting room at the depot chain their baggage to one of the seats. Many pieces of baggage were noticed secured this way at the Union Depot yesterday.
May 29

-Officer Nichols yesterday killed a dog on Missouri avenue which was supposed to have been mad. Jack Gallagher ought to be let loose on the town before long, or at least before the dog days.
June 5

-Persons residing in the vicinity of Elmwood Cemetery complain that the Sabbath is desecrated and the peace disturbed in that neighborhood by young bloods, who come out from the city and indulge in horse racing. It is also of frequent occurrence on week days, a race having been run yesterday and considerable money put up on the result.
June 11

-Isn't it about time for something to break loose in the city. This thing of no murders, sensations or fires is getting to be monotonous to the reporter.
June 13

-A few days ago Abraham Lincoln paid a fine in the Police Court, and yesterday morning George Washington also paid one. Both were colored and the charge was intoxication. Neither of them

claimed to be related to their illustrious namesakes.
June 13

-The Board of Health have ordered that no more dumping of refuse and dirt into the river shall take place, just west of Broadway along the river front. The stench from that quarter is sickening and is caused by throwing the offal, etc., into the water at that point.
June 15

-Yesterday was the last day allowed for the taking of the census. Those who have not been taken will have to remain unnumbered among the people of the United States for the next ten years.
June 16

-The commencement exercises of the graduates of the High School are to take place on Thursday evening at the Board of Trade Hall and will consist of essays, declarations, orations and music. The graduates this year are fifteen young ladies and five young gentlemen and Miss Montgomery is to deliver the valedictory.
June 16

-Several of the school houses in the city are to be enlarged ere long. The Lathrop is to be expanded by three or four rooms; the Woodland by two, and a new building to be known as the Kansas School, containing six rooms is to be built on Troost avenue between Third and Fourth streets. The cost of the

improvements will be about $20,000.
June 17

-In the Public School Library, which is under the auspices of the Board of Education, there are nearly 2,000 volumes. Any style of work wanted can be found, except the lower class of fiction. All the leading magazines are received, and any one can go to the Board of Education rooms and read to their heart's desire. The price of a membership is only $2 per year. It is an excellent library, and the terms are very low. Let reading people examine it, and its membership will soon be doubled.
June 17

-River rising rapidly, drift running, and sandbar disappearing.
June 18

-Indians on the street yesterday caused small boys to be late at school.
June 18

-It is now understood that Gen. Grant will reach this city on Friday morning, July the 2d, over the Chicago, Rock Island & Pacific Road from Des Moines.
June 18

-The street cars leaving now every two minutes is a great accommodation to those living in the bottom.
June 19

-Six hundred and twenty cases have been before the Police Court since the beginning of the fiscal year, April 19.
June 19

-The Grimes building, on Delaware street, has been selected by the Grant Reception Committee as the place for holding the banquet, on Friday night, July 2d.
June 19

-Considerable excitement was manifested yesterday on Ninth street, West Kansas, by a man riding his mule into James McCue's saloon, where he ordered a quart of beer, which the mule drank, and his owner taking a smile backed his animal out and rode away.
June 19

-At Jack Gallagher's slaughter yesterday morning nineteen dogs were doomed. One old New Foundland dog, seeming to understand what was being done followed the executing officer around the pen, imploring mercy as well as it could with its dumb language. It was the last killed, and the sight made some of the spectators turn away with tears in their eyes. Two dogs were sold for $2.30, and two hogs for $1.80.
June 20

-There is talk among the sporting fraternity of organizing a bicycle club in this city.
June 23

-The building being erected by Mr. Brocklein at the corner of Broadway and Fifth streets has been discovered to be on the spread, and yesterday workmen commenced to take down the top story, which will leave the building two instead of three stories as originally intended. The loss will be considerable.
June 23

-John Muehlbach, a well known brewer of Kansas City, died last night at his residence, corner Eighteenth and Main streets. He was fifty-six years old.
July 2

-In the Circuit Court yesterday S. G. Biglow and F. M. Shaw entered suit against Kersey Coates and the Mastin Bank for $4,000 on two bills of exchange on the National Park Bank of New York for $2,000 each.
July 11

-A gentleman while getting shaved at the Union Depot barber shop fainted away from the extreme heat yesterday, causing quite a commotion for some time.
July 12

-A number of funerals took place yesterday, more than usual. Every hearse in the city was engaged in conveying the dead to their last resting places.
July 12

A Slice of the TIMES

-Nellie Goodrich, colored, for occupying a room for prostitution, was fined twenty-five dollars, and C. C. Cook, white, for cohabiting with her, and frequenting a bawdy house, was fined six dollars. The arrests were made by Capt. Malloy and L. W. Gent on Monday night. The fines were paid in both cases.
July 14

-A child of M. Brown's of West Kansas, only fourteen days old, was seized with lockjaw yesterday.
July 20

-A large two-story building is in process of erection on Ninth street, near the State line, to be used as a day and night school for those who cannot attend the public schools, and for an industrial school for girls. On Sundays mission services will be held. The matter is in the hands of Hon. Geo. M. Shelley, E. L. Martin and C. W. Chase, and will be made a success. It is a very important thing for the citizens of West Kansas.
July 21

-Esther Clark, alias Campbell, for keeping a bawdy house, was fined by Recorder Finney $27.00, and each of the three inmates of her establishment paid into the city treasury $7.00.
July 24

-Some parties spread the report yesterday that the Santa Fe Road wanted to hire 500 men and the office at the Union Depot was besieged from morning till night. The rumor, however, had no foundation.
July 24

-Four cars of provisions have been sent from Kansas City to the Kansas suffers. This is about 54,000 pounds, representing $2,500. There are still other collections to be heard from.
July 27
These provisions were for the newly arrived "exodusters."

-Vegetables and garden truck of all kinds are so cheap, that a small family can live on about fifteen cents a day, provided the meat and bread can be obtained on tick.
July 29

-Several large droves of hogs came in yesterday for Plankington and Armour. The heat killed quite a number on their way from the Stock Yards.
July 29

-The heat was so intense yesterday that everything wilted. In some places in this city birds were picked up that had died from the effects of sunstroke.
August 1

A Slice of the TIMES

-Yesterday morning the alarm of fire was sounded in New Town, the colored settlement opposite the Stock Exchange. Being on the south side of the Kaw River two small shahties were burned before the flames were extinguished. Burning brush near one caused the trouble, and the loss is about $30.
August 4

-The colored citizens had a big time in the city yesterday and last night. The occasion being the third annual conclave of the Independent African Grand Commandery. A grand street parade was made by the order yesterday, and an installation of officers took place last night.
August 5

-George and John Muelhback are preparing to build a large two-story brick brewery, corner of Main and Eighteenth streets, at a cost of about $20,000. The machinery will cost $14,000.
August 7

-Madam Luck, the notorious bawdy house keeper on Grand avenue, was up before United States Comissioner Wyne, yesterday, charged with selling liquor without a license. She was bound over in the sum of $100 to appear before the United States Circuit Court.
August 7

-Eighteen cases were before Recorder Finney yesterday morning. Fourteen of these were common drunks, three peace disturbers, and one for carrying concealed weapons.
August 11

-Ed. H. Webster will answer to the Recorder this morning for violation of the fire ordinance in erecting a small wooden stable in the rear of his real estate office on Main street. Mr. Webster proposes to contest the right of the city in the premises as he has a building permit.
August 17
Mr. Webster was fined $25.00 for the violation, and insisted he would appeal.

-George Williams, a colored man, erected a wooden building on Sixth and Campbell streets, contrary to the city ordinance, and yesterday the Recorder fined him $26. The building will be taken down and the fine remitted.
August 25

-Some dissatisfaction has been expressed regarding Policeman Ragan's shooting at the negro Gregg at the Union Depot Monday night, and yesterday he was suspended. He will be examined ᴜiis afternoon before the Board of Police Commissioners.
August 25

A Slice of the TIMES

-Undertaker Weldon recently purchased a new hearse, which arrived Wednesday. It is of the latest style, with gold and silver plated plumes, and the inside gold embroidery on black broadcloth. It is said by good judges to be the finest establishment of the kind in the West.
August 27

-Three very notorious lewd women were before the Recorder yesterday morning, for street walking. Josie Sheppard was fined $11, Sallie Williams $26, and Tenny Jones $21, and they all went to the workhouse.
August 29

-Wm. Lamberdon was yesterday fined $25 for erecting a wooden building contrary to the fire ordinance. These cases are becoming very frequent of late, and the City Engineer proposes to prosecute every violator of the ordinance, without regard to who he is, as it was passed for the benefit of the entire city.
August 29

-"Hell's Half Acre" is partially under water.
August 30

-A great many cellars are reported full of water from the recent rains.
August 30

"Exodusters" - 1880

-Happy Hollow is filled with water and the denizens of that classic locality leave their homes in boats.
August 30
"Happy Hollow" was a poor residential section of the city bordered by Broadway and Washington, Sixth and Tenth streets.

-It was reported yesterday that the Fair Grounds property had been sold to Boston capitalists for $2,000 per acre.
September 2

-The amount of rain for the month of August, as reported by Mr. J. P. Kenmier for the TIMES, has been extraordinary, twelve and twenty-six one hundredths of an inch having fallen. During the last week in the month nine and twenty-one hundredths of an inch fell, which is the largest for any week during the year.
September 2

-Dennis Ragan was arrested by Officer McCorkie yesterday morning, for stealing a pair of boots from Mr. J. Rudd's store on Main street. The fellow had them under his coat when captured, and said he "just wanted to try them on." Mr. Rudd will not prosecute him, and a charge of vagrancy was set opposite his name.
September 3

A Slice of the TIMES

-An old-fashioned four-ox emigrant team passed through the city yesterday, and attracted considerable attention.
September 8

-It is said that Will E. Baker, of the Journal, is to be city editor of the new evening paper and that Frank Clark will fill the vacancy on the Journal.
September 14
The "new evening paper" the reporter is referring to is the "Kansas City Star."

-The crowds at the Fair Grounds yesterday were very large, probably not less than 12,000 people being there during the day.
September 20

-The hotels of Kansas City, although there are many and the accommodations large, will be crowded during the week and their capacity tested as never before.
September 20

-The streets were crowded with people last night.
September 24

-Business at all the county offices was yesterday suspended, the officials enjoying the day at the fair.
September 24

-Yesterday afternoon a fellow with a couple of tin boxes, with which he played a game similar to the old fashioned thimble trick, was brought in off the fair grounds, but as he begged earnestly and said he had not "worked" any one during the entire week, Chief Speers gave him an hour to leave town, and he did not let the grass grow under his feet as he left the station.
September 26

-The new Lathrop school was opened yesterday; also the two new rooms of the Woodland school. The rooms were filled with children as soon as opened and the accommodations are as yet hardly adequate to the demands. The schools throughout the city are reported as progressing finely, with an unexampled attendance.
September 28

-The city physician, Dr. Jenkins, has opened an office on Fifth street, between Main and Walnut streets.
September 30

-The wheel of fortune men were tried before Justice Ranson, yesterday, and fined $10 and costs each, amounting to about $150. They were E. W. Scott, Billy Campbell, B. Johnson, R. R. Lewis, L. A. Harper, J. T. Wright and Thomas Hanford.
September 30

A Slice of the TIMES

-Since the establishment of the Kansas City Free Dispensary on East Eighth street, near the corner of Main, a number of people have been treated. Any one who is poor and worthy of assistance will be treated free of charge by calling at the office between 11 in the morning and half past 1 o'clock in the afternoon.
September 30

-Ex-Mayor Shelley has opened a wholesale dry goods store on West Fifth Street, and reports business booming. The first day he opened he received twenty-three orders from his old customers, and is highly pleased at his prospects. No man in the city has more friends than George Shelley, and they will all be glad to learn of his merited success.
October 1

-Beer kegs appear to be terribly in the way of pedestrians on Twelfth street, West Kansas. Yesterday morning Henry Brewster walked into a pile of them, which upset him into the gutter, barking his shins and dislocating his wrist.
October 2

-Officers Hasse and McGinniss made a raid on a tent on the levee yesterday, and took one man and two women to the station on the charge of living in a bawdy house.
October 4

"Exodusters" - 1880

-Ann street, which extends from Seventh to Ninth, between Delaware and Wyandotte streets, will no longer be known by that name. The city council last night passed an ordinance, introduced by Ald. Dragon, changing the name to the more euphonious one of Amarette.
October 5

-A colony of about sixty colored people went out to Nicodemus over the U. P. road yesterday.
October 7

-The difficult task of cleaning the immense chimney at the Union depot was completed yesterday. Almost four wagon loads or soot was the result of the job.
October 15

-The meeting of Catholics, called at the old court house for last evening to make preparations for the reception of Bishop Hogan, was largely attended. The matter of reception was warmly championed by all present, and a committee was appointed to prepare an address, to be delivered on the occasion of the visit of the bishop, and the meeting adjourned.
October 18

-The representatives of the various newspapers interested in forming a Press Club in Kansas City, met yesterday afternoon in the TIMES office. The meeting was informal, and nothing of importance

was done. An adjourned meeting will be held in the parlors of the St. James hotel, Tuesday evening, for further discussion of the matter.
October 18

-Yesterday afternoon a boot black of stout build and having quite a fancy box appeared on Union avenue, stating he was going to cut rates on the boot blacking business. The words were no sooner out of his mouth than a dozen of the "regulars" pitched into him, and the drubbing he received will lay him up for some days to come. A metropolitan was required to restore order, which he at last did.
October 19

-At last something is going to be done to make the wards of the City Hospital more comfortable. Last evening the city council passed an ordinance appropriating money to build a wall under the male ward and plaster the interior, beside making other improvements. This should have been done some months ago.
October 19

-Two new saloons are getting ready to open on Ninth street, West Kansas. This will make twenty in about two blocks.
October 21

-A very sensational report of the passing of the James boys through Kansas City was published in the Star last evening. These boys know when they

are well off and give this city a wide birth.
October 22

-Maggie Ford, a little girl ten years old, was fined
by Recorder Finney $5.50 yesterday morning for
assaulting and dragging another little girl around by
the hair of her head.
October 23

-The Kansas City Press club will meet this
afternoon at 3 o'clock, in the editorial rooms of the
Star, for the purpose of adopting a constitution and
bylaws. A full attendance of the reporters is
requested.
October 24

-At the Morse school there are children of ten
different nationalities in attendance.
October 26

-Nothing but politics was talked about upon the
streets yesterday.
October 31

-A barricade was built yesterday in front of the
window at the City Hall, where the Fourth ward
voters will cast their ballots to-day.
November 2

-Business has been resumed with renewed vigor
since the election.
November 5

A Slice of the TIMES

-The epizootic does not seem to increase in violence, and the horses suffering from it are improving.
November 5

-The council will meet Monday night in special session. One of the measures to be under discussion is the elevated railway.
November 6
This was a planning session for what would become the "Ninth Street Incline," a railway to continue Ninth street down, over the bluffs, to the West Bottoms and back.

-The rumor that the prohibition law had carried in Kansas has caused preparations to be made near the State line on Ninth street for the erection of four buildings for saloon purposes.
November 6
The saturation of saloons in this area eventually led to it being known as the "wettest block in the world." 23 out of the 24 buildings were saloons.

-Many are grumbling at the slow pace the street cars are run, but the mules being all effected by the epizootic necessitates this, and it is only by the greatest of care that Superintendent Corrigan keeps matters running at all.
November 6

-The District Telegraph department of the Bell Telephone company is now in working order throughout the city. Instruments are being put up in various localities and in every way the system extended.
November 9

-The Exposition company have re-leased the same grounds they formerly occupied for five years longer. The price is about the same as before, but they are obliged to relinquish a number of privileges they formerly held. Several locations were offered the company, but they decided not to purchase as long as the present grounds could be leased.
November 12

-It having been suggested that the press association of this city give an entertainment Thanksgiving night for the benefit of the poor of the city, there will be a meeting of the newspaper men at the office of the Evening Star this afternoon at 3 o'clock to discuss the matter, and if thought feasable, to make arrangements for the same.
November 14

-A dog fight on Twelfth street, West Kansas, yesterday, drew a crowd of nearly 400 people.
November 15

A Slice of the TIMES

-The city council meets to-night in special session. The Ninth street elevated railway will come up for consideration, as well as other important ordinances.
November 15

-Diphtheria is again raging. Thursday night, W. H. Kattlewell, living on Locust, between Fifteenth and Sixteenth streets, lost two children by the dread disease. They will be buried to-day, by Undertaker Welden, in the same casket.
November 20

-There were many happy families in Kansas City, and many who ate the best dinner they have had for a year, thanks to the generosity of the citizens and the labor of the Press club.
November 26

-The condition of Father Donnelly is about the same as for the past three or four days, there being no perceptible change. The best of care is given him, and everything that can be done for his comfort is being done by the Sisters, at whose hospital he is.
November 26

-The public barnyard, by courtesy called a square, was the scene of much stir and business enterprise yesterday. Among others there was the noisy stationery vender and the man who lets you pound a post for five cents a stroke.
November 28

242

-Rankin, the inventor and manufacturer of artificial ice, was in the city yesterday. He stated he was now manufacturing ice for forty skating rinks, and could manufacture ice for skating purposes with the thermometer at 70°, sufficiently hard for use.
November 29

-The streets were slippy yesterday morning, very slippy, and the profanity that resulted from this fact was of a volume and variety that required the best efforts of the divines to counteract yesterday. The spectacle of a lot of "won't go home till morning" gentlemen climing up Ninth street hill on their hands and knees, was one of the amusing incidents which greeted the newspaper man homeward bound at an early hour.
November 29

-The squatters in tents and rude cabins along the river front, in various ravines and hollows about the suburbs, have suffered greatly from the prolonged cold weather which has struck this part of the country at this unusual season. In some instances little children living in these places have been badly frost-bitten.
November 30

-The river is very low, there being only about six feet of water in the channel at the bridge.
December 2

A Slice of the TIMES

-Ice dealers have staked off the river bank, and are laying claim to the frontage thus marked off. Those who have been counted out of good cutting territory are disposed to dispute the claims.
December 2

-There is something radically wrong at the central office of the Telephone company. After 8 o'clock in the evening it is almost impossible to get communication with anyone through the medium of the telephone.
December 2

-A number of poker rooms have recently been opened by the sporting men who have lost their occupations by the closing of the regular faro rooms.
December 3

-The action of the Council in abolishing the tramp's room is strenuously objected to by the business men of the city.
December 9

-It is said the salutes fired by the Grand Army of the Republic broke about $100 worth of glass in various parts of the city. Rather costly advertising.
December 9

-There is an increasing demand for a morgue in this city.
December 11

"Exodusters" - 1880

-Father Donnelly is failing fast. A few hours more and he will be at rest.
December 12

-The members of the Salvation army begin to appear in numbers on the streets.
December 14

-There is no truth in the report that the Mastins are about to pay all their obligations and resume banking with a capital of $1,000,000, or pay any other sum. The assignee of the bank has paid 17 cents on the dollar, and claims are now selling at 8 to 81/2 cents. To pay out and resume would require a capital of about $2,000,000, which the boys haven't got.
December 17

-There were 169 carriages in the Donnelly funeral procession yesterday. All along the route the walks were lined with people to see the procession pass, some of whom had waited several hours. The damp weather and muddy roads prevented hundreds from joining the procession on foot.
December 18

-The flames were scarcely extinguished at the corner of Main and Missouri avenue, yesterday morning, before the excavation was begun for the foundation of a new brick building, which will be erected over the old shells that have occupied that corner.
December 23

A Slice of the TIMES

-The city was full of country cousins yesterday who came in to spend Christmas with their friends.
December 26

-The shooting was good over on the sandbar yesterday. Two hundred and ten shots were fired at one turkey, and then boys knocked his head off with a club.
December 26

-There are now 165 mules in the Jackson county street car stables. They eat up one ton of hay daily, besides 1,000 bushels of corn, 400 bushels of oats, and two tons of bran monthly.
December 26

-The tramp room has been abolished, and on such nights as the last the poor and homeless must steal to get lodgings at the station. This looks like offering a premium for crime. The honest man or woman must freeze outside, while the thief enjoys a warm fire. "Oh, for the rarity of Christmas charity."
December 28

-Farewell to the old year. A greeting to the new.
December 31

Epilog

George Consider Hale, the enterprising inventor and fireman, was appointed as Chief of the Fire Department by Mayor Thomas Brockway Bullene in 1882. For the next twenty years, he continued to improve efficiency in the department and patented over ten of his fire fighting inventions. Two of his most important inventions were the Hale Water Tower, an extendible hose and nozzle that could direct a stream of water directly into a building six stories high, and the Hale Swinging Harness which could be secured to a horse in from one and three-quarters to three seconds time. In 1893, Hale led his department to victory in a world-wide fire fighting competition at the International Fire Congress in London. They won every event. With George Hale's improved methods and time-saving equipment, the Kansas City Fire Department was able to do in seconds what in took others minutes to complete. In 1900, with the help of their fastest horses, Buck and Mac, Hale's Department took first prize again at the International Exposition in Paris.

George C. Hale's affiliation with the Fire Department came to a abrupt end the evening of April 21, 1902. Under a cloud of political friction between Hale and Mayor James A. Reed, the Mayor called for the support of the Upper House of the City Council in removing Hale from the Fire Department. Unspecified charges of insubordination, misrepresentation and conduct unbecoming an officer were raised against Hale at the City Council meeting that evening. After some debate, the vote was taken and Hale was dismissed. He remained good-natured, however, and returned that night to fire department headquarters to say good-bye. He was met by the grim faces of his men. They had already heard the news. "Do you boys know anybody that's got a job for me?" he shouted to the group. Only a few faint smiles was the response.

A Slice of the TIMES

Hale retired. In 1915, over 1,200 cards were signed asking George C. Hale to run for Mayor, but apparently he wanted nothing to do with politics. He died July 14, 1923.

Major George Newton Blossom, who went from managing the "eating stand" at the Union depot to caretaker of its upper rooms for travelers, took out a building permit in the fall of 1880 to build his own hotel on Union Avenue across the street from the depot. The "Blossom House," opened in 1882 and quickly became one of the most elegant and popular hotels in the area. Major Blossom died on August 27, 1885, after having been a resident of the city for only eight years, but the hotel retained his name. When train traffic was re-routed to the new Union Station and the old depot closed in 1914, the Blossom House, as well as many other hotels in the area, found it could no longer remain open, and shut its doors forever January 1, 1915. The building was torn down in 1920.

Former Alderman Edward Kelly, owner/operator of the Mechanics' Hotel on 9th Street in West Kansas, lost out to James Pendergast in a bid for control of First Ward politics (formerly the sixth ward) in 1885. Always an astute business man, he began buying land and building houses during the real estate depression of the late 1880's and early '90's. He built two apartment complexes known then as the "Kelley Flats," one of which encompassed an entire block near 16th and Paseo. When he died at the age of 88, he was collecting payments on promissory notes from the sale of 19 separate properties.

Ex-Mayor George M. Shelley, generous to a fault, continued to operate his successful wholesale dry goods company, later known as the Western Mercantile Company, and remained politically

Epilog

active. But the man who, as mayor, had given all of his salary to charity or public improvements and started what would become the Mayor's Christmas Tree Fund to feed the poor, was forced to file for bankruptcy in 1910. The failure of several businesses which Shelley had sponsored years earlier in the amount of $200,000, forced him to devote nearly all of his salary as collector of water rates to pay down the debt. He had all but $72,000 paid off when he finally gave in. "I could have become a voluntary bankrupt years ago, but I wouldn't," he told a Kansas City STAR reporter in 1927. "But now I'm getting old; there's no use denying that - and I couldn't do it any longer." He estimated that he had loaned about $1,600,000 to people, many of them politicians, during the time since he was mayor. "I lent money to everybody; almost," he said. He never got any of it back. Shelley was not soured by the ordeal, however, and spent the next nineteen years trying to recover. He died after a fall coming down the stairs of his office, January 6, 1929, at the age of 81.

Shelley Park, also known as Cemetery Park and the "little dornick on the East Side," was doomed from the start. The descendants of the original Old Town proprietors, led by Edward L. Scarritt, filed suit against the city for possession of the land in 1882. Public opinion ran against the heirs, but for the next twenty years they remained firm in their demands. When it was feared the group might win on the argument that the land had been given to the city as a public cemetery thus the conversion of the property was illegal, the city had tombstones and monuments placed around the grounds. But in 1902, the final decision of the State Supreme Court was made in favor of the Old Town heirs. That same year a group of club women chose the site as the city's first playground for children, and later it was used as a ball park. The heirs formed the "McCoy Land Company" in 1908 and built a row of shops on the Independence Avenue side. By the late 1920's, all the park property had been built on. Today, the Southeast corner is covered by a highway ramp and a new firestation sits on the remainder of the site.

By 1875, steamboats and river packets were already on the decline. The Missouri River had always been a risky route. Snags, or floating trees, were a common occurrence and led to the destruction of many boats. The river's swift currents and sharp bends smashed others onto the shores. But nothing ensured the downfall of the steamboats more than the railroads. The railroads brought not only safer, more direct delivery of supplies to the west, but the railroad bridges built across the rivers made navigation even tougher for the packets. After run-ins with the bridges in Boonville and Kansas City, the steamer Joe Kinney smashed into the Glasgow bridge on April 13, 1882. She was a total loss. On August 7, 1882, the boilers of the packet Gold Dust exploded just outside of Hickman, Kentucky, killing seventeen and wounding forty-seven. An account of the tragedy appears in Mark Twain's "Life on the Mississippi." In 1883, the Kate Kinney was lost to fire at Shreveport, Louisiana.

The colorful personalities of "Burnt Faced Mary," "Mormon Ann," "Crazy Alice" and others, faded from the scene as increased industrial development in the west bottoms engulfed "Hell's Half Acre." By 1901, "that classic locality" had become the subject of nostalgic reminiscence.

Bibliography

-----*Kansas City Times*. January 1, 1875 - December 31, 1880

-----*A Memorial and Biographical Record of Kansas City and Jackson County, Mo.* Chicago: The Lewis Publishing Co. 1896

Ballenger & Hoye's Kansas City Directories. 1875 - 1880

Brown, Theadore A. *Frontier Community.* Columbia, Missouri: University of Missouri Press. 1963

Brown, Theadore A. and Lyle Dorsett. *K.C. - A History of Kansas City.* Bolder, Colorado: Pruett Publishing Co. 1978

Case, Theodore S. *History of Kansas City, Missouri.* Syracuse, New York. D. Mason. 1888

Deathrage, Charles P. *Early History of Greater Kansas City.* Kansas City, Missouri: Interstate Publishing Co. 1927

Dorsett, Lyle W. *The Pendergast Machine.* New York: Oxford University Press. 1968

Green, George Fuller. *A Condensed History of the Kansas City Area - Its Mayors and Some V.I.P.s.* Kansas City, Missouri: The Lowel Press. 1968

Jensen, Malcolm C. *America in Time.* Boston: Houghton Miffin Co. 1977

Bibliography

Ladwig, Craig, Editor. *The Star - The First 100 Years.* Kansas City, Missouri: Kansas City Star Co. 1980

Reddig, William M. *Tom's Town - Kansas City and the Pendergast Legend.* Philadelphia: J. B. Lippincott Company. 1948

Sandy, Wilda. *Here Lies Kansas City.* Kansas City, Missouri. Bennett Schneider Inc. 1984

Schlesinger, Arthur M. Jr., Editor. *The Almanac of American History.* New York: G. P. Putnam's Sons. 1983

Wheeler, Mary. *Steamboatin' Days - Folk Songs of the River Packet Era.* Baton Rouge, La.: Louisiana State University Press. 1944

Wilson, William H. *The City Beautiful Movement In Kansas City.* Kansas City, Missouri: The Lowell Press, Inc. 1964

Worley, William S. *J. C. Nichols and the Shaping of Kansas City - Innovation in Planned Residential Communities.* Columbia, Missouri: University of Missouri Press. 1990

Mounted newspaper clippings files of the Missouri Valley Room, Kansas City, Missouri Public Library, 311 E. 12th Street

252

Index

Index

160, 173, 185, 202, 212, 214, 228, 231, 232, 233, 239
Cross, Asa Beebe, 3, 30
Crossings - See *Sidewalks*
Currency, 67
Davis, Officer, 155
Dog Licensing, 192, 194
Eclipses, 63, 165
Edison, Thomas A., 97, 161, 181, 185
Education - See *Schools*
Electioneering, 48, 61, 62, 63, 70, 71, 72, 74, 87, 89, 90, 91, 92, 93, 97, 148, 150, 173, 174, 186, 208, 239
Electric Light, 181
Emigration West, 2, 13, 18, 19, 55, 58-59, 79, 125, 185, 234
Execution, 146
Exodusters, 208, 210, 212, 213, 214, 217, 218, 219, 221, 229, 237
Exposition, 31, 32, 36, 87, 88, 161, 189, 241
Farrel, John, 51-52, 205
Fashons, 148, 173, 210
Father Dalton, 46, 105, 145, 147
Father DeSmet, 59
Father Donnelly, 242, 245

Fire Department, 2, 8, 22, 24, 34, 39, 47, 68, 171, 176, 189, 197, 247-48
Fire Ordinance, 231, 232
Fires, 7, 9, 16, 36, 106, 116, 139, 204, 219, 230
Foster, Frank, 47
Fountains
    Drinking, 2, 138, 162, 199;
    Ornamental, 2, 17
Frank's Hall, 53, 143, 178, 179
Freeman's Hall, 153
Freedman's Record, 76
Gallagher, Jack, 192, 193, 194, 196, 200, 202, 204, 213, 219, 221, 223, 226
Gambling, 2, 93, 95, 126, 140, 153
Gardner's Billard Hall, 75
Gas Company, 9, 10, 41, 106, 130, 131, 134, 135, 141, 156, 213, 220
German Population, 68
Ghosts, 44, 82-83, 148
Globe Hotel, 133, 140
Grain Trade, 29, 51, 98, 101, 108, 122, 146
Grant, General Ulysses S., 225, 226

Index

Index

Index

Prairie Schooners - See *Wagons*

Press Club, 124, 237-38, 239, 241, 242

Prostitution, 2, 15, 23, 84, 85, 101, 121, 228

Public Square - See *Market Square*

Quality Hill, 1, 21, 30, 34, 38, 70

Railroads, 2, 146, 205, 250; price war, 32, 33; Atcheson, Topeka & Santa Fe, 37, 53, 55, 58-59; Missouri River, Fort Scott & Gulf, 50, 60-61, 116, 125, 166, 221

Rice, John, 180

Riverview Park, 111, 117, 197

Roller Skating, 104, 102, 105

St. Patrick's Church, 17, 18, 30, 46

St. Teresa's Academy, 31, 38

Sawyer, Judge, 40, 57

Scanlan, Andy, 39

Scarlet Fever, 130

Scarritt, Edward L., 250; Nathan, 139

Schools, 23, 28, 37, 39, 68, 70, 87, 100, 123, 152, 203, 218, 224, 224-25, 225, 228, 235, 239

Sewers, 2, 82, 88-89, 92, 109, 116, 121, 133-34, 158, 163, 164, 196, 198

Shelley Park, 2, 44, 152, 153, 156, 172, 175-76, 249-50

Sheridan's Pond, 110, 198, 201, 202-03

Sidewalks, 1, 38, 114, 126, 140, 158, 174, 197, 211, 215; crossings, 51, 133, 140, 156, 206, 209, 210, 212

Slavens, Mansur & Co. - See *Meat Packing Industry*

Sledding, 100, 101, 179, 182

Sleighing, 96, 98, 99, 100, 177, 180

Small Pox, 151, 152, 160

Speers, Thomas M., Chief of Police, 110, 235

State Line Depot, 55, 113, 118, 127, 150

State Line Resurvey, 70, 81

Steamboats, 75, 109, 157, 250; Arabia, 133, 171, 172; Ashland, 195; Benton, 43; Fannie Lewis, 38, 219, 169;

257

Index